strategy.applied

Waking the Giant

Revitalising the mature brand

PETER
STEIDL

WILEY

First published 2009 by
John Wiley & Sons Australia, Ltd
42 McDougall Street, Milton Qld 4064

Office also in Melbourne

Typeset in Adobe Caslon Pro 11.5/14.5pt

© Peter Steidl 2009

The moral rights of the author have been asserted

National Library of Australia Cataloguing-in-Publication entry:

Author:	Steidl, Peter.
Title:	Waking the giant : revitalising the mature brand / Peter Steidl.
ISBN:	9781742169521 (pbk.)
Notes:	Includes index.
Subjects:	Branding (Marketing)
	Branding (Marketing) — Management.
Dewey Number:	658.827

Printed in China by Printplus Limited

10 9 8 7 6 5 4 3 2 1

Disclaimer

CONTENTS

Part III: selecting the strategy that's right for you   149

ACKNOWLEDGEMENTS

Some five years ago I co-authored a self-published book on the revitalisation of mature brands with Kim Boehm, a long-standing friend and colleague, then Managing Director at Young & Rubicam Melbourne. It was great writing with Kim, but he has since taken up the position of Managing Director at Clemenger BBDO Adelaide and I found myself facing the challenge of mature brands alone this time.

Much has happened since our earlier collaboration. In particular, there are three aspects I have given special attention to in this book. First, I note that it is not uncommon for executives to mix elements of a revitalisation strategy with a milking strategy. This is not likely to work. It is therefore important to go through a proper evaluation of the merits of these alternative strategies and to then make a decision either to milk or to revitalise.

Second, there is extensive research that shows that strategy development is often not the key issue. Rather, the problem is implementation. More often than not, mature brands are owned by mature companies—companies that use outdated processes and tools, being able to absorb inefficiencies and second-rate strategies because of their size and market power. It makes sense to identify and eliminate work practices that foster a brand's maturity before focusing on strategy development. There is little point in implementing a revitalisation strategy while, at the same time, the company continues to work with out-dated processes and tools that accelerate maturity.

Third, I felt that strategy selection deserves special attention. It is, actually, not that difficult to identify a range of revitalisation options. It is much more difficult to select the strategy or bundle of strategies that will deliver the best return.

The result is, I hope, a reasonably comprehensive and useful perspective on the revitalisation of mature brands.

While my name is on the cover, there are a number of parties who have contributed in significant ways. As mentioned, Kim Boehm has been my partner-in-arms at my earlier attempt to address the revitalisation of mature brands; Vija Blumbergs has tirelessly reviewed early drafts and provided advice on structure and focus; my colleague Valerie Lim prepared relevant case studies.

Geoff Wild, Chairman of WPP Group (Australia); Kathy Keele, CEO, Australia Council; Kathy Barber, General

Manager—Consumer & Market Insights, Foster's Group Ltd; and Glenn Myatt, Group Marketing Manager, Underwear & Hosiery Group, Pacific Brands, reviewed a draft manuscript and provided feedback and encouragement.

Raja Kanniappan, Group M's CFO Asia–Pacific and Chairman of the Editorial Board of the Strategy.Applied series supported my effort absolutely; John Petropoulos and Mark McCraith, both senior Mindshare executives, allowed me to dedicate time to write this book. Importantly, I want to thank my publisher, Katherine Drew, who championed the project within John Wiley & Sons, and the Wiley team that has contributed significantly to the book you now hold in your hands.

Finally, I want to acknowledge my indebtedness to the many experts, marketing practitioners, academics and consultants who have undertaken groundbreaking work that has allowed me to learn more about the revitalisation of mature brands. My gratitude goes to them and to my clients who have allowed me to contribute to their own revitalisation efforts, creating learning opportunities for me.

This is the second book in the Mindshare Strategy.Applied series, published by John Wiley & Sons. Management is about managing change and, given the rapidly changing environment, many executives find that short-term quarterly results and day-to-day challenges absorb so much of their day that it is difficult to set time aside to think about broader strategic issues. The Mindshare series aims at providing management with easy-to-read, focused input addressing some of the major challenges they face.

This book is an attempt to deliver on this promise. I hope I have succeeded and thank all those who have helped me on the way.

Dr Peter Steidl
April 2009

We are in the middle of a recession. One might well ask: why write a book on the revitalisation of mature brands at a time when the focus in most companies is on adapting to the recessionary environment rather than implementing grand, long-term strategies?

There are a couple of reasons for this.

In my recent book on recession strategies, *Survive, Exploit, Disrupt: action guidelines for marketing in a recession* (John Wiley & Sons, 2009), I pointed out that times of significant change make it easier for corporations to disrupt the way they are doing business. In many organisations, a recession disrupts conventional marketing practice as the company responds to revenue and margin pressures by cutting costs, simplifying processes, and discontinuing marginal product lines or high-cost innovation programs.

These adaptations and changes are typically erratic, as they are reactive rather than proactive. This is not a criticism. It is near impossible to predict how the market and competitive environment will change during a recession, so companies have to continually adjust their strategies, structures and processes in response to often unexpected and dramatic changes in the operating environment.

However, a revitalisation program can provide a positive focus that shapes the actions taken in response to pressure. For example, when cutbacks are required and processes and structures need to be streamlined, the company can use this opportunity to eliminate outdated practices that constitute barriers to a revitalisation effort. As I will demonstrate in this book, many companies spend significant budgets on activities that prevent, rather than support, the revitalisation of their mature brands. Eliminating these is a highly desirable first step towards achieving growth with stagnant major brands.

There is a second, more personal reason for addressing this topic. The maturity of leading major brands is one of the great mysteries of the marketing world. Of course, we can point to the life-cycle concept showing that brands do eventually mature and decline, but we have to keep in mind that this concept is descriptive in nature, that is, it simply reflects what typically happens, rather than providing any compelling reasons as to why maturity and decline have to happen in the first place.

Similarly, the now widespread concept of tracking the market position of brands based on extensive databases is largely just describing what is happening. The analysis may well be able to identify how a brand's strengths, relevance or relationships with consumers are changing over time, but these are just indicators that the brand is progressing towards maturity, rather than providing an insight into the drivers of these changes or any conclusive proof that maturity is inevitable.

It almost appears as if our acceptance of the life cycle is clouding our judgement and compelling us to accept maturity as inevitable, rather than encouraging us to address the question of how we can avoid maturity through effective revitalisation strategies.

Having always been attracted to exploring how to break conventions, this is an attempt at addressing the mystery of maturity. In many major corporations — especially those competing in developed markets — brand maturity has become part of everyday life.[1] So much so, in fact, that it is often just accepted as a reality that can't be changed.

Fortunately, today we have a much better understanding of maturity, its underlying reasons and how to revitalise mature brands.

Marketing has a proud history of 'borrowing' from other professions and disciplines. Not surprisingly, much of what we have learned about the revitalisation of mature brands over the last few years has come from such diverse sources as industry economics, the neurosciences, corporate strategy and psychology.

However, this knowledge is fragmented. Despite my intense interest in this topic I was not able to find a single, focused publication that brings together the different

---

1 I am specifically focusing on major brands that have moved into the maturity or even decline stages of their life cycle.

streams of learning into actionable guidelines for the key decision makers, the custodians of the brand.

This book attempts to bridge that gap.

In this book, I cover the key developments, insights and learnings that are essential to the development and implementation of a successful brand revitalisation strategy. To keep the resulting publication to a manageable size that doesn't put off busy executives (the very target group I have in mind), I naturally have had to be selective and sometimes a little superficial. However, I hope that this publication will help brand custodians to develop and implement considered and effective brand revitalisation strategies.

The book has been structured into three parts.

Part I: making the commitment

Commitment grows out of necessity, or at least a firmly held belief that a particular strategy is in fact the most effective way of generating the desired returns.

In chapter 1, I discuss how revitalisation is not always the best option and it is important that the key alternative — applying a cash-cow strategy to the mature brand — is considered before embarking on a revitalisation program. To this end I explore the respective benefits of milking versus revitalisation.

Clearly, a highly effective strategy that is not implemented as intended won't deliver the expected benefits. Implementation accounts for the difference between idea and innovation, between budgets on a spreadsheet and money in the bank, between dream and reality. Yet, as David Maister suggests in his book *Strategy and the Fat Smoker*, we all know what we need to do, but don't do it.[2]

Given that in most organisations it is implementation where failure occurs, I start with this issue rather than presenting it as an afterthought. After all, a willingness to implement the strategy is the most important commitment that needs to be made.

In chapter 2, I encourage you to abolish work practices that contribute to—and perhaps even cause—the maturity of your brand. There is little point in allocating resources to the implementation of a revitalisation strategy while continuing with work practices that accelerate maturity.

Chapter 3 advocates the adoption of new work practices that deliver flexibility and ingenuity, and tools that provide meaningful and reliable input into key decisions.

Finally, I highlight the need for executives to adopt a different thinking mode—one that fits the environment we manage in today. This operating environment is faster, more complex and less predictable than ever before. We need to review the way we think and thus reach decisions. Most likely we will find that our approach to thinking is very much in tune with the past, that is, an operating environment that was ultimately more predictable. This observation has significant ramifications.

---

2 D Maister, *Strategy and the Fat Smoker: doing what's obvious but not easy*, Spangle Press, 2008.

Part II: revitalisation strategies

In the second part of the book I turn my attention to the development of a revitalisation strategy. A number of strategic options are presented. It is important to note that these are not recipes for success, nor have I put together something like 'The 10 Immutable Laws of Revitalisation'. The truth is that there are no recipes when it comes to management. Change is the order of the day and what worked yesterday doesn't necessarily offer us a way forward today.

The strategic options I present are not mutually exclusive. In fact, they cover a wide range of core approaches. Again, believing that there is no single best approach, I feel it is important to present the reader with a variety of options. I hope that some of the concepts, tools and ideas presented will take you on a new path, allowing you to see your mature brand challenge from a different perspective, leading to fresh solutions.

Part III: selecting the strategy that's right for you

The third and final part of this book deals with strategy selection. More specifically, when a number of strategic options have been identified, how can the most effective one be identified for implementation? Undoubtedly, there will be a host of internal factors that will force the elimination of some options — budget restraints, technical feasibility and risk adversity, to name just a few. However, it is important that the remaining options are also considered in light of the ever-changing operating environment.

First, you need to ensure that your brand revitalisation strategy is aligned with your industry's evolutionary path. Importantly, if you already experience a lack of alignment (which could in fact have contributed to the maturity of your brand), your challenge is to select a strategic revitalisation option that allows you to close this gap.

Second, you need to be in tune with tomorrow's consumer, rather than follow industry conventions that look at consumers through the rear-vision mirror. We all know that consumers are changing, but the change is accelerating and, given that your revitalisation strategy needs to be effective in the future, you need to understand the key drivers of change and factor these in when evaluating your strategic options.

I close by stressing the need for the strategy to have sufficient impact to break through the barrier of indifference mature brands typically face in the marketplace.

If I manage to offer you just one or two ideas, concepts, tools or fresh approaches that change the way you manage your mature brands, I will have succeeded. If you read this book with interest but don't make use of what I am presenting, then I have failed.

PART I

MAKING THE COMMITMENT

A G Lafley, Procter & Gamble's CEO, famously said: 'Products have life cycles; brands don't'.

Of course, brands do follow a natural life cycle. However, unlike a product, a brand can be revitalised. A poorly managed brand will reach maturity and decline, but a well-managed brand won't, unless the company cannot muster the ingenuity, resources or commitment needed to revitalise it. Lafley's statement can be looked at as a challenge to the marketing community from the CEO of the world's most successful diversified FMCG (fast-moving consumer goods) company, rather than a statement of fact.

At the same time, Lafley would have been the first to demand that the revitalisation of mature products should not be automatic, but should be considered against the alternative strategy of milking the mature brand. Both strategies are often feasible and it cannot be assumed that revitalisation is always the better option. Clearly, the ultimate decision between 'revitalise' or 'milk' will be made in the context of the brand portfolio and alternative investment opportunities open to the corporation. However, this higher level corporate decision can only be made on the basis of an exploration of these alternative brand strategies.

For this reason we will start our revitalisation journey with the all-important question: revitalise or milk?

Regardless of which strategic path it is to be, commitment to the adopted strategy is imperative. A mix between revitalisation and milking is not likely to succeed. It will not deliver the financial returns a milking strategy should generate, and it will be too watered down to be effective in revitalising the brand.

While commitment to a revitalisation strategy is essential, however, it is not sufficient to succeed. Too many companies commit to a revitalisation strategy, but then fail to implement it as intended. Instead, as the implementation process unfolds, the strategy is adapted again and again by various parties who need to contribute to the effort. This is not a case of executives or staff deliberately undermining the strategy. Rather, it tends to be the result of applying outdated criteria, processes and procedures that invariably weaken the strategy until it is hardly distinguishable from the company's typical run-of-the-mill approach.

Work on the concept of ingenuity suggests that hiring ingenious employees does not necessarily lead to an ingenious organisation. In fact, these employees may be totally ineffective if they are straight-jacketed by traditional processes and procedures that don't accommodate change and that kill innovation. The same applies to the revitalisation of mature brands: a highly effective strategy won't help if you are not prepared to also ensure that it will be implemented as intended.

The most surprising aspect is that despite the many adaptations made during the implementation phase, executives may still expect the strategy to deliver the hoped-for results. Naturally, it will fail to deliver these.

While outdated work practices are invariably at the root of the implementation problem, it is often worse than that; many corporations employ work practices that accelerate, if not cause, the brand's maturity in the first place. In the surreal world of these corporations we find resources allocated to a revitalisation strategy while conventional work practices continue to accelerate the brand's maturity. Needless to say, this is utterly counterproductive.

Abolishing outdated work practices is arguably one of the most difficult challenges faced by organisations. While executives typically agree that the operating environment has changed dramatically, they seem to fail to make a connection between their work practices and these external changes.

Marketing is, in particular, guilty of resisting a change in work practices. Consider the massive changes in manufacturing that have taken place over the last 20 years—not just manufacturing technology, but the integration of the total supply chain, changes in the organisational structure, the multitude of new processes that are often self-organising in nature, the skill mix of those working in this functional area. We don't see changes in marketing anywhere near those we can observe in manufacturing.

Sometimes it appears that marketing has been caught in some sort of time warp. We all know that some 80 per cent of new products fail and that the vast majority of these have been researched prior to launch. Yet we continue to use the same outdated research methodologies. Can we really expect different results? As Albert Einstein said, 'insanity is doing the same thing again and expecting different results'.

Why do marketers adhere to lengthy planning cycles while agreeing that the rate of change is accelerating and even the short-term future is becoming less predictable? Why are they using conventional research methods that have failed over the last 30 years to deliver the deeper insights required to develop effective strategies? Why are analytical methods such as brand pyramids and brand wheels still being used when it is widely acknowledged that we need to create and manage an integrated experience? Why is the effectiveness of marketing communications measured on the basis of recall when we know today that exposure to an ad can change brand perceptions without the consumer being able to recall the ad? Why is the use of digital media opportunities often limited to simply transferring traditional exposure methods into the digital space rather than generating true engagement with the consumer?

This is not a book about work practices. But we need to at least highlight some of the work practices that represent barriers when it comes to successfully implementing a revitalisation strategy.

But there is light at the end of the tunnel. Let's return to Procter & Gamble (P&G). As AG Lafley reports, under his leadership P&G has adopted new market research practices, and changed external and internal relationships, structures, processes and the company's strategic focus. P&G's focus shifted from attempting to generate growth from new brands and acquisitions to the revitalisation of the big, mature brands in P&G's stable. And Lafley succeeded beyond all expectations.[1] So can you. But, as I said earlier, an effective revitalisation strategy is essential to but not sufficient for success. There must be commitment to making it happen. With this in mind, I hope you will find the following section of interest.

---

1   AG Lafley & R Charan, *The Game-Changer: how you can drive revenue and profit growth with innovation*, Crown/Random House, 2008.

CHAPTER 1

BEFORE WE START, IS IT REALLY WORTH THE EFFORT?

By definition, major mature brands lack growth but they nevertheless may still enjoy strong market positions. While margins and growth opportunities are typically less than exciting, it is possible that a significant return can be extracted over time by managing the brand's decline effectively.

A milking strategy that focuses on margins rather than volume, by investing just enough to extend the profitable life of the brand, is often a viable alternative to a revitalisation strategy. However, while both alternative strategies—milking and revitalisation—should be considered, once a choice has been made it is vital to stick to the chosen strategy and adjust short-term as well as long-term expectations to ensure these are aligned with the strategic choice.

OCCUPIER BRANDS

By definition, major mature brands occupy quite strong positions in their established markets. In fact, we could call these brands occupier brands, because their strength is typically not based on differentiation and brand loyalty but on the territory they have occupied in the past and the well-established habitual buying patterns of consumers.

This position is typical for the leading brands in many categories and markets. Major banks, retailers, petrol companies, FMCG brands and many others derive much of their strength from a past where differentiation and astute marketing have allowed them to occupy significant market territory.

For brands like these, the question 'Why bother with a risky revitalisation strategy when we can milk the strong market position of our mature brands?' is not an idle one.

A commoditised market, that is, a market where brands lack differentiation, typically benefits the major players. When there is no meaningful differentiation from the market's perspective, consumers tend to buy major, well-known brands rather than brands with a low profile. They also tend to stick with their purchasing habits, rather than spend energy and time going through a decision-making process. After all, there is little apparent gain in evaluating their purchases when they see little difference between the options on offer.

Why bother with a risky revitalisation strategy when we can milk the strong market position of our mature brands?

The only problem is that while major, mature brands tend to enjoy a significant market share in a commoditised market, unfortunately commoditisation destroys value. Margins get thinner as the market increasingly buys on the basis of price and convenience, reducing revenue and increasing costs. Fortunately for many mature brands, there have been significant developments in many areas—from manufacturing to communications, from service to logistics—that have allowed companies to reduce their costs. Think internet banking, the relocation of call centres and manufacturing to low-cost countries, advances in manufacturing technologies, efficiency gains in transport (in particular air and sea) and warehousing, productivity gains due to software and the associated improved information and transaction flows.

Importantly, these benefits tend to be far more significant for large-scale organisations than for their smaller competitors, thus typically benefiting the 'major mature brand' organisation.

This is, of course, the trap: major mature organisations tend to be quite profitable and they appear to make significant progress in terms of efficiency and associated profit gains. In fact, they have most likely refined their internal processes, systems and procedures to be highly efficient, so they can extract the maximum competitive cost advantage from their large scale of operation. On the downside, they have limited their flexibility by aligning the operation totally with their existing strategy, thus building barriers to any significant change in strategy.

IN FAVOUR OF A MILKING STRATEGY

Returning our focus from the broader organisational perspective to the brand itself, we need to explore the concept of 'occupied territory' further.

... we are primarily interested in ... the reasons for the brand's ability to hold on to its strong market position despite its maturity.

I have already mentioned that major mature brands tend to maintain their market share rather well, despite their lack of growth. But, while we can use market share as an indicator of the size of the brand's territory, we are primarily interested in the factors underlying market share, that is, the reasons for the brand's ability to hold on to its strong market position despite its maturity.

Some of the factors that may allow a major mature brand to maintain a strong market position are:

- *Familiarity*—the mature brand typically enjoys a high degree of familiarity, which is important in commoditised markets. After all, familiarity is the basis of forming habits. An extreme case of familiarity is a situation where the brand name starts to be synonymous with the category. For example, many consumers ask for 'Kleenex' when they want a facial tissue or for 'Coke' when they want a cola drink.

- *Share of relationships*—in many industry sectors major mature brands have built a wide range of customer relationships that constitute barriers to exit. One of the most widely used strategies is the implementation of a loyalty scheme, including the ubiquitous loyalty card. These schemes work particularly well when purchase or usage determine a particular membership status. For example, would a member of a frequent flyer program risk their Gold or Platinum status by flying more often with another airline?

But even an increase in relationships based on multiple product use, such as a customer using multiple banking products, reduces the likelihood of change, as a change becomes a more significant and potentially messier step to take.

- *Power over distribution channels or proprietary distribution channels* — A brand that has a strong position in a distribution channel can limit competitors and, quite often, build barriers to make it impossible for competitors to enter these channels in the first place. Major brands such as Coca-Cola, Cadbury, Kraft, Kellogg's and Nestlé have such strong positions on supermarket shelves that it is extremely difficult for new competitors to get shelf space.

  In the case of proprietary distribution channels, these channels can become a major factor in keeping customers and obtaining new customers, due to the importance of convenience and visibility in commoditised markets. It is also likely that the company has established outlets in some of the best locations, thus pre-empting moves by would-be competitors.[1]

- *Share of partnerships* — a brand can extend its sphere of influence and keep competitors out of its territory

---

1 Proprietary distribution channels can fortify a company's position, but because of the associated high fixed costs they may become a weak spot when a competitor successfully employs a disintermediation strategy (that is, implements a business model that does not require physical outlets).

by building partnerships with complementary organisations (for example, banks with retailers). Potential partners tend to prefer getting into bed with a major brand, even if it is mature, because of the immediate benefits such a brand brings with respect to customer base, market coverage and brand familiarity.

An emerging or challenger brand may well have a promising future, but relying on future developments is risky and the benefits are longer term. For example, it is no surprise that petrol companies have entered into partnerships with major retailers, regardless of how mature they may be. It is obvious that a similar partnership with a smaller retail chain would not be as attractive from the petrol company's point of view.

As there are invariably only a small number of desirable major partners, signing one of them up makes it more difficult for others to achieve competitive parity. In other words, major mature brands — as the preferred option — can typically sign up with the most powerful partners, further solidifying the position they hold in their territory.

- *Ingrained habits* — by 'training' customers to do things in a particular way, the brand can build barriers to change. For example, supermarket customers like to go to the same supermarket every time, not because they think it's a 'better' supermarket, but because it is easier for them to find the products they are looking for, once they are familiar with the layout. In a recent consulting assignment, I recommended the development of symbolic icons to a supermarket chain that would help customers to navigate and find items faster. Such a proprietary symbolic language has the potential to keep customers loyal even when moving to another area or while away on holidays.

Similarly, customers who are not adept at the use of computers resist a change to another bank once they have mastered the internet banking facility of their current bank.

The same principle often applies to product brands: once consumers have mastered their Apple computer they prefer to stay with Apple; once they are conversant with their Nokia mobile phone, they are more likely to buy this brand again if the features and functionality are familiar.

Flavour sensations tend to be even stronger than just ingrained habits. There is no doubt that consumers get used to particular flavours, which is what makes it so important to recruit young people and build them into life-long customers. It's no wonder that Pepsi and Coke both aim at the younger segments, rather than at reinforcing the drinking behaviour of older age groups.

> *... a proprietary symbolic language has the potential to keep customers loyal even when moving to another area or while away ...*

And Cadbury has a proud history of getting young consumers used to the particular chocolate flavour it offers across the leading products in its range.

- *Suppliers* — the development of a network of superior suppliers can allow a competitor to gain significant efficiencies and advantages when it comes to quality and reliability. These supplier networks are of critical importance in many industries.

At the same time we note that a strong supplier can in fact drive commoditisation by focusing the market's attention on the 'ingredient' provided, as is the case with Intel. This brand has become such a trust mark that even a lesser known computer brand may be considered simply because it offers 'Intel inside'.

These are just some examples of how major mature brands have occupied territory that allows them to defend their strong market position even after they have lost differentiation. It is important for a mature brand to survey the territory owned, as there may well be strategic opportunities that have not yet been exploited.

So, why bother with revitalisation when things are working for the major mature brand? There appear to be many good reasons for the major mature brand to continue finetuning and improving its existing operation, without worrying too much about disruption and change. After all, the mature brand appears to be in a commanding position.

IN FAVOUR OF A REVITALISATION STRATEGY

There are two key reasons the mature brand needs to consider revitalisation strategies. The first reason is that ⁓ve innovation by a competitor, possibly even a tional one, could eventually destroy the very basis ture brand's success.

Consider the case of Encyclopaedia Britannica which was beaten by online encyclopedias, or the dent Dyson made in the upper end of the vacuum cleaner market through revolutionary new technology—a market that had prev- iously been dominated by Electrolux.

One day a challenger brand may emerge, based on a disruptive product or business model innovation, and the major mature brand that has refined its performance, aligned its processes, built huge legacy systems, and tailored its infrastructure to what has suddenly become an outdated business model will suffer.

So, to come back to the core of our argument, when price and convenience become significant factors in a purchase decision-making process, it is typically the dominant brand that has the advantage. This is due to cost efficiencies that come with scale and experience, a solidified position (the best locations, extensive shelf space, and so on) and significant resources, including free cash flow.

When we look at the equation from the consumer's point of view, we can see that the cost of change—that is, changing to a competing brand—is often a deterrent. This cost is not necessarily financial in nature. It includes the need to work out where things are in a different supermarket, or the time required to fill out forms and go through an identity check when changing from one financial institution to another. Given the perceived lack of differentiation, why would a customer willingly accept this cost just to get the 'same' again?

The well-established mature operator also has the advantage of being able to use what could be disruptive innovations as sustaining innovations. For example, online banking and grocery shopping are by nature disruptive, disintermediating innovations. However, when these potentially disruptive innovations are integrated into existing operations, they become sustaining. This means they support the current operation and thus eliminate the potential competitive threat a dedicated operator might have presented by establishing a specialised position. Put in simpler terms, when 'your' supermarket offers online shopping or 'your' bank offers internet banking, why change to some online specialist newcomer?[2]

Clearly, mature operators typically have the financial strength and/or share market valuation to allow them to acquire start-ups that enter the market with potentially disruptive innovations. These can either be integrated into the current operation as sustaining innovations (see above), or be run as separate organisations. This allows the mature operator to quickly move up the experience curve with respect to the disruptive innovation, while building barriers to entry for newcomers who want to ride into the market on the back of such an innovation.

It is worth noting that Amazon was arguably only successful because the major mature book retailers were slow to implement their own online strategies. Barnes and Noble, in particular, could have offered a bricks and mortar network combined with an online facility, which would have been far superior to Amazon's offer. But

---

2   Things are not quite as straightforward from the business model point of view, as the newcomer is likely to focus on a part of the value chain where significant cost advantages can be extracted—even while having scale disadvantages (for example, a specialised online banking competitor with a small customer base versus a major retail bank). We will deal with these disintermediation strategies in a later section.

presumably due to its reluctance to compete with its traditional distribution channel, Barnes and Noble did not respond quickly; when it did respond, it was initially in a half-hearted way. This allowed Amazon to fully develop a disruptive innovation—buying books online—that provided a real alternative to industry convention. The same innovation would have been sustaining for Barnes and Noble had it capitalised on it.

In fact, a 'brick and click' network exploiting the synergies between on- and offline would have been far superior to the offer by a specialised online operator. You could use the stores as a point to return books you did not want after all. The stores could also have started to pursue corporate business more aggressively, becoming advisory centres and working with staff development consultants and human resource specialists online as well as offline, staging seminars, workshops and so on.

Traditional bookshops could have morphed into learning and entertainment centres. Instead, all the major chains did was add some coffee shops while essentially sticking with their old strategy (which was undoubtedly highly refined and efficient) while a specialist online competitor started to gain market share.

So, as we can see, in a commoditised market there are many factors that typically favour the major, mature brand. But sticking with the mature brand strategy means accepting the risk of a competitor launching a disruptive innovation that renders the 'old' business model ineffective. At the same time we note that the development and implementation of a revitalisation strategy also creates risk. If revitalisation were an easy task we would not have any mature brands.

I said earlier that there are two reasons a revitalisation strategy may be the best answer when dealing with a mature brand. The first reason, covered above, is the threat of a disruption by a competitor.

The second reason is that it will get increasingly difficult for the mature brand to satisfy its shareholders without investing in a revitalisation strategy. This is because the expected future growth is already factored into the share price. To improve the share price further thus requires outperforming the market's expectations. This is rarely possible by continuing to deliver efficiency gains. Significant efficiency gains have typically already been extracted and, while continuous improvements are important, they will not lead to a major step-wise improvement that will significantly affect the share price. New breakthrough innovations are typically non-proprietary and, due to the price sensitivity of commoditised markets, efficiency gains will largely be passed on to the consumer through price competition.

... it will get increasingly difficult for the mature brand to satisfy its shareholders without investing in a revitalisation strategy.

REVITALISE OR MILK?

In summary, we have two options: milk the mature brand or embark on a revitalisation strategy. What is critical is that we need to make a strategic decision in favour of one or the other. A 'mixed' strategy that leads to a limited investment into revitalisation while not fully exploiting the milking opportunities is likely to fail.

So, what is it to be: revitalisation or milking?

The title of this book may suggest that I recommend the revitalisation of mature brands at all cost. Nothing could be further from the truth. Sometimes the best decision is to manage maturity effectively rather than to revitalise. By treating mature brands like cash cows we may in fact get a very sound return on investment (ROI) from these brands in the medium term, perhaps even long term, while slowing their decline.

A cash cow strategy is often misunderstood as an approach that extracts the maximum possible cash flow from a brand while killing it off. That is a 'dog' or 'exit' strategy, not a cash cow strategy.

The cash cow strategy demands an investment into the brand — more specifically, an investment that is sufficient to extend the profitable lifetime of the brand. The cash cow strategy is typically a medium- to long-term strategy and has little to do with the short-term exit strategy that should be applied when dealing with a dog brand.

Often, both revitalisation and milking are viable options. While it may seem more desirable to revitalise a mature brand, it is sometimes a much better strategy to milk it. I have already stressed that 'milking' does not mean sucking it dry. A milking strategy is based on the principle that you invest as much as necessary to keep the cash cow alive. However, invest no more than you expect you will be able to extract as returns from your investment over the cash cow's expected lifetime.

Typically it is appropriate to increase or at least maintain the price even in light of a falling price level in the category, as margin is more important than volume. This means focusing on buyer segments that are prepared to pay a somewhat higher price because they are either loyal to the brand or simply don't care about paying a bit more. It follows that price promotions are used less often and promotions that emphasise the value of the brand need to be dominant. This may allow you to extract a significant free cash flow from this brand over its remaining lifetime and, in many instances, this will be measured in years rather than just months.

Revitalisation is only a better option when there is reason to believe that you can create a stronger market position for the brand, allowing you to achieve not only an ROI that beats the corporate hurdle rate over the brand's extended lifetime, but that is also higher than the ROI expected from a milking strategy.

Clearly, the choice between a revitalisation strategy and a milking strategy will also have to factor in alternative investment opportunities (hence, you need to consider the corporate investment hurdle, which would have been set in light of the portfolio of investments open to the company).

A problem arises, however, when an executive pursues a dog or cash cow strategy but expects the revitalisation of the brand to occur.

I will explore the many ways executives may damage their brands in a later section. Let's just briefly refer here to price promotions, value packs, discount vouchers, specialling and other strategies that destroy the position of the brand and educate the consumer to become more and more price-focused. These and similar initiatives are akin to an exit or dog strategy, and one cannot expect them to result in the improved returns of a milking strategy.

Similarly, one cannot expect the revenue growth a revitalisation strategy offers from a milking strategy. Recently a major food company asked me to confirm that they had done everything that could be done to achieve growth with a particular FMCG brand. My investigation showed that the client was clearly — and very effectively — pursuing a cash cow strategy. After an initial period of heavy price promotions and value packs the client had switched to a cash cow strategy, discontinued the value packs and maintained a high price.

... one cannot expect the revenue growth a revitalisation strategy offers from a milking strategy.

In line with the typical cash cow strategy, there was a lack of innovation or fresh thinking. The target market, the value proposition, the communications strategy and just about any other element of the marketing mix was pretty much the same as it had been over the last decade. Clearly, there was a cash cow strategy rather than a revitalisation strategy in place, yet the client believed that the actions taken should somehow revitalise the brand.

This situation is not uncommon and may well have to do with executives getting so close to the day-to-day marketing task that they can't see the bigger picture. There is obviously a danger when expectations and actions are not aligned.

THE MONOPOLY BRAND

I have referred to the major mature brand as an 'occupier brand', as its strength comes primarily from the territory it has occupied over the years. There is, in fact, a special type of occupier brand that we need to consider because it differs in important aspects from the major mature brand we typically find in commoditised markets. This is the monopoly brand.

The monopoly brand is still significant in many markets. This brand is typically mature and lacks growth, but dominates specific markets. However, unlike occupier brands, monopoly brands have not had to fight for the territory they occupy, but were given that territory through legislation. Typical examples can be found in utility, transport and telephony markets that have not yet been deregulated or that are currently going through a period of deregulation.

Deregulation obviously affects the position of these brands. Like the occupier brand, they defend their territory. However, unlike the occupier brand, it is deregulation that allows other brands to enter what used to be an exclusive domain.

I believe there are significant similarities in market position between the occupier brand and the monopoly brand that is affected by the process of deregulation: both have a strong market position due to the territory they occupied in the past.

But there are also significant differences when it comes to strategy development. The monopoly brand that

is transitioning due to deregulation can either go
fortification or plan an organised retreat from territory tl
is being thrown open to competition through legislation.
Meanwhile, the occupier brand may not be able to foresee
which part of the occupied territory will be most at risk.

Most importantly, the occupier brand typically faces at least
one if not several competing occupier brands, while the
monopoly brand has a unique position in its marketplace.
It will undoubtedly face new competitors, but they cannot
match the experience base, infrastructure and solidified
position the monopoly brand enjoys in its traditional
market(s). For this very reason, deregulation often imposes
restrictions on the monopoly brand, limiting it in the use
of its competitive strengths.

The custodians of monopoly brands who find themselves
in a deregulated environment may find the guidelines in
this book valuable.

KEY POINTS

- In many categories mature brands are still
  dominating the market despite their lack of positive
  differentiation. This dominance is partly due to
  consumers' habits and partly due to the territory
  these brands have managed to occupy:

  ○ Habits are a powerful determinant of consumer
    behaviour in an undifferentiated, commoditised
    market.

  ○ The occupied territory includes share of
    awareness, relationships and partnerships, as well

as dominant roles with respect to distribution channels and suppliers.

- Given the strength of the major mature brand in the marketplace one might well ask, '*Why bother* with a revitalisation strategy?':

  o First, when the brand is not living up to its full potential, a revitalisation strategy may be able to generate revenue and profit growth.

  o Second, a mature brand is a sitting duck—sooner or later a competitive brand will launch a disruptive product or business innovation and change the rules of the game in the industry sector. A revitalisation strategy pre-empts such a move by competitors or reduces, or even neutralises, the damaging impact of a competitor's disruptive strategy.

- However, it is important to consider the relative merits of a cash cow strategy before embarking on a program of revitalisation:

  o 'Milking' the brand means optimising the profit contribution this brand makes over time by investing sufficient resources to prolong the profitable life of the brand.

  o Such a strategy requires discipline; the marketer needs to be strong rather than succumb to price promotions and other initiatives that destroy the value of the brand.

- Both alternatives, milking and revitalisation, should be considered. However, once a decision has been made in favour of one or the other, the marketer needs to stick to the chosen strategy and adjust short-term as well as long-term expectations to ensure these are aligned with the strategic choice.

CHAPTER 2

ABOLISH WORK PRACTICES THAT CAUSE MATURITY

Arguably the most common reason for the maturity of major brands is the commoditisation of the category. A market is commoditised when the consumer fails to see any meaningful differentiation between brands due to a perceived lack of difference in what these brands offer.

Given the importance of commoditisation when dealing with maturity, it makes sense to ask, 'How do markets commoditise?' Surely, it is not some magical event that just happens. Marketing executives don't wake up one morning and find to their astonishment that the markets that are the lifeblood of their brands and careers have commoditised overnight.

Sadly, it is invariably the industry itself that drives commoditisation. History would suggest that it is human nature to avoid risk and to think short-term, and ways of doing this are:

- mixing tactics and strategy
- taking a process-driven approach to brand strategy planning
- copying what other successful operators are doing
- reducing the risk and cost of innovation by buying and using third-party technologies
- offering more new features nobody wants to know about
- simply delivering what the consumer asks for.

Clearly, there is little point in investing in a revitalisation strategy if, at the same time, the company engages in work practices that are accelerating commoditisation. Following is a brief overview of some common commoditisation drivers. You need to seriously think about abolishing any of these practices if they are typical for your company.

MIXING TACTICS AND STRATEGIES

Competitive pressures cannot—and should not—be ignored. However, you will never revitalise your brand if your marketing program is largely reactive, comprising a never-ending series of reactions to competitive pressures. Revitalisation typically demands differentiation. Differentiation can hardly be achieved when managing in a reactive mode.

Many industries today are characterised by a heavy emphasis on price promotions and on the frequent release of a multitude of product variations. These are not innovations, just simple variations such as different flavour combinations, different sizes, different colours and different feature combinations. These are usually reactive strategies; the objective is to match competitors to ensure they don't gain market share by employing these tactics, or to give the communications program something to talk about.

... you will never revitalise your brand if your marketing program is largely reactive ...

Such tactics are rarely sufficient to revitalise mature brands. In fact, the contrary effect can be expected: the commoditisation of a product market accelerates when mainstream competitors engage in price promotions and the frequent release of marginal new product features that constitute only small improvements (this will be discussed further in a later section). Tactical price promotions train the consumer to be more price-conscious, thus placing less emphasis on any features that may differentiate brands. The frequent release of incremental product improvements reinforces the view that all competitors offer more or less the same products and performance benefits, giving the consumer no basis for the development of true brand preference.

I recognise that it is difficult for a marketing director to keep a clear, long-term strategic focus when daily competitive pressures are threatening quarterly results. It is therefore important to embed the difference between strategy and tactics into the organisation. This can be done by appointing a senior marketing staff member, reporting to the marketing director, who takes responsibility for tactical responses. Delegating tactical response decisions to a senior member of staff allows the marketing director more time to focus on the challenge of revitalising brands and on sustaining their re-energised positions.[1]

Another approach is to establish a strategy review board that brings senior executives together to review marketing programs from the strategic point of view. This can also be a valuable means of bringing together a wider group of stakeholders, such as executives from R&D, sales, logistics, finance and other disciplines. A well-run strategy review board may even be attractive to a busy CEO, facilitating direct access to the key decision maker and an opportunity to position marketing as a strategic discipline that can have a significant impact on future financial results.[2]

A well-run strategy review board may even be attractive to a busy CEO...

In any case, a strategy review board or similar institutionalised review and advisory body highlights the importance of strategy in a visible and powerful way. It is important, however, to stress that we are not talking about delegating the most important strategic branding issues to a committee. The board provides the ultimate marketing decision maker with an opportunity to get input and feedback from a wider audience comprised of relevant experts who, more often than not, also need to play an important role when it comes to the implementation of a

---

1   We recognise that delegation is difficult for many senior executives, especially when it comes to issues of immediate concern. While marketing directors may agree that tactical issues are rarely of long-term importance (unless not addressed at all), they nevertheless tend to favour involvement in what is urgent, even if this means neglecting what is important.

2   Bruce Tait has the following comments to offer: 'Marketing Directors and CMOs need to think about repositioning the marketing department, since it seems to be slipping in importance in most companies. CEOs need to come to see this department as the source of business-building ideas—a distinction it seems to have lost in most cases.' (B Tait, 'How "marketing science" undermines brands' in *Admap*, October 2004, pp. 48ff.)

brand strategy. This should allow for impr
as well as a smoother strategy implemen
But the strategic decision remains in
director's domain.

Benchmarking: copying what others are doing

In the 1980s, Peters and Waterman published their much celebrated book *In Search of Excellence*.[3] In this book, the authors presented the then leading companies, together with their analysis of what made them so successful.

As senior executives typically find it difficult to resist a simple recipe, it comes as no surprise that many companies adopted the same sorts of approaches, concepts, values and processes that allegedly made these companies so successful. This is despite the fact that, only a few years later, many of these 'excellent companies' had fallen into disrepute, had disappeared or were struggling, clearly demonstrating to the world that what works depends on the environment one competes in. There are no absolute strategies that always work. But ignoring this simple corporate fact, benchmarking — the rather naive idea that 'if it worked for them, it will work for me' — was off the starting blocks and seemed unstoppable.

Naturally, it didn't take long before consultants and academics turned their minds to the development of benchmarking services as a means of generating fee income. The multitude of workshops, consulting services

3   TJ Peters & RI Waterrman, *In Search of Excellence: lessons from America's best-run companies*, Harper Collins, 1982.

and benchmarking programs added to the perceived credibility of this approach and accelerated its spread through many industry sectors.

Unfortunately, most benchmarking simply encourages imitation. And imitation leads to a lack of differentiation. And a lack of differentiation leads to commoditisation.

Benchmarking does make sense under certain conditions:

- an inferior competitor, focusing on indicators that reflect efficiencies rather than strategic performance

- a me-too brand that has no ambitions beyond copying the leader

- a competitor undertaking strategic benchmarking outside its own industry sector.

However, benchmarking is often used by mainstream competitors to benchmark their performance against other mainstream competitors. A set of indicators is selected which determines the focus of the benchmarking effort. These indicators implicitly become internal performance indicators that focus management's attention on specific performance aspects, determining success and failure on the basis of how well the organisation is performing vis-a-vis its major competitors.

Clearly, this situation encourages imitation. When a competitor is doing well in a particular performance area (say, the number of transactions handled by its checkouts) and we want to achieve the same level of performance, we will investigate *how* the competitor achieves the superior results—and then we copy this approach. As long as we focus on efficiency in our benchmarking the results may not be disastrous, although the alignment of our processes, systems and procedures with those implemented by competitors will limit the degree of strategic freedom we enjoy. Once we start benchmarking in areas that relate to effectiveness — and in particular when we are dealing with aspects of strategy — we are clearly in danger of contributing to the commoditi-sation of the industry. Whenever we copy a strategy or approach taken by a competitor we accelerate commoditisation.

Non-proprietary technologies driving innovation

The fact that the technologies that drive product innovation are often not proprietary doesn't help either. There is a story that has been told a million times because it makes the point: Which company facilitated the building of skyscrapers? If you are straining to think of building or architectural firms, don't bother. The answer is: Otis. Without the development of elevators we would not have seen skyscrapers. This technology was offered to any developer or builder who was happy to pay for it, and thus allowed a multitude of parties to build skyscrapers.

Whenever we copy a strategy or approach taken by a competitor we accelerate commoditisation.

Today we find that innovation in many industries is driven by non-proprietary technologies. Take banks, for example: ATM, internet banking, credit card operations, cheque-clearing software are not any particular bank's proprietary technology. In all these cases we find that the underlying technologies are owned by third parties or, sometimes, industry consortia.

As companies attempt to increase their efficiency by buying in innovations rather than developing them in-house, they limit their ability to differentiate themselves through innovation. Procter & Gamble is widely known for its leadership role in marketing. However, P&G has invested heavily over many decades into proprietary manufacturing technologies and processes that allow the company a strategic flexibility and cost efficiency that serve as strong differentiators.[4]

... there must be some capability or asset that differentiates your firm.

In many product categories it is near impossible for competitors to meet P&G's unit costs or unique product features, delivered by advanced, proprietary manufacturing solutions and capabilities. This provides P&G with a competitive advantage that may not be sustainable, but—as P&G has demonstrated over a long time—is certainly renewable.

The lesson is clearly this: there must be some capability or asset that differentiates your firm. If that's not the case you will be struggling to gain and then constantly renew a competitive advantage.

Meaningless, incremental innovation

Clayton Christensen[5] argues that product innovation cannot drive differentiation once the product's performance

---

4   See K Grichnik & C Winkler with J Rothfeder, *Make or Break: how manufacturers can leap from decline to revitalisation*, strategy+business series, McGraw Hill, 2008, pp. 140ff.

5   CM Christensen, *The Innovator's Dilemma*, Harvard Business School Press, 1997; CM Christensen & ME Raynor, *The Innovator's Solution*, Harvard Business School Press, 2003; CM Christensen, SD Anthony & EA Roth, *Seeing What's Next*, Harvard Business School Press, 2004.

exceeds market requirements. This argument is, of course, convincing. Why would consumers spend money on a product improvement if the product's performance already exceeds their needs?

Clearly, once performance exceeds consumer need, product innovation loses its impact in the marketplace. Consider the many product categories where this has happened, from tyres to radios, washing machines to air-conditioners, personal care products to cars.

Figure 2.1: product innovation loses effectiveness when category performance exceeds market expectations

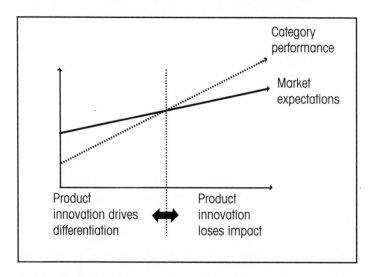

I am not suggesting that differentiation is impossible. However, product innovation becomes less effective as a differentiating factor that sets a product apart from its competitors in a *meaningful* and powerful way.

Let's look at mobile phones as a specific example. Every few months competitors introduce new, incremental features presumably designed to create brand differentiation. The market, however, simply becomes more confused and generally doesn't want to know about the dozens of features a product offers. The results of recent surveys conducted by Nokia, Microsoft and IBM suggest that consumers or buyers of quite different products share one attribute: they don't want feature overload and, in fact, they only use a small percentage of the features already available with the products they own.

The market is more likely to respond favourably to the occasional breakthrough feature that makes a real difference in the way the product can be used or in what it delivers. For example, the ability to take pictures changed the role a mobile phone plays in the user's life. The only problem now is that the camera option has quickly become a feature offered by all the major brands.

Von Braun, in his classic book *The Innovation War*,[6] also suggests that the regular launch of new, but not groundbreaking, features confuses the market. Today's consumer is too blasé about technological progress; any new features have to add significant tangible or intangible benefits and have to be easy to comprehend. Consumers will not spend their time learning about new product features. Rather, they ignore them, convinced that they don't need the new features anyway and that, furthermore, these features will soon be mainstream, offered by all major brands. In short, they convince themselves that the product category is commoditised.

---

6   CF von Braun, *The Innovation War*, Prentice Hall, 1997.

Von Braun also looks at the internal impact of frequent, incremental innovation versus major, infrequent but disruptive (or at least step-wise) innovation. There are many factors that make frequent incremental innovation quite unattractive. These include shortened product life cycles and the resulting need to amortise development and tooling costs over a shorter period of time, and the cost of frequent model run-out sales that have to be staged at lower cost simply to make room for the 'new' model in the retail channels. The message here is to consider the total cost of incremental innovation to the business, not just the R&D costs.

... consider the total cost of incremental innovation to the business, not just the R&D costs.

On the positive side, I note that *positioning* innovation based on regular product innovation can be a viable strategy once category performance exceeds market expectations. What I am referring to here is a brand positioning that is based on innovation, that is, creating a brand that stands for innovation. In archetype terms we are talking about the creator brand. Apple is, of course, a creator. Consumers choose Apple because it is a brand that stands for innovation, rather than because of a specific, single product feature. But for most corporations and product categories, emulating Apple would be a lofty, possibly unachievable, goal.

The good news is that positioning innovation does not rely only on product innovation to give it substance. A brand that is positioned as an innovator can demonstrate its personality and qualities at any touchpoint. For example, the brand can innovate at point-of-sale, or by creating different distribution channels (the pop-up shop, for example, is still an innovation that seems to get attention). Other touchpoints are its marketing communications, sponsorships, brand activation and so forth.

DELIVERING WHAT THE MARKET IS ASKING FOR

It may come as a surprise that delivering what the market is asking for is a factor that leads to commoditisation. On the other hand, you must have heard the saying, 'If you don't develop a strategy for yourself, you become part of somebody else's strategy'. This is essentially what happens when you let consumers decide your future.

Conventional marketing wisdom was to go to consumers, find out what needs or problems they have, and then solve them. But I believe that this approach needs rethinking. Consumers have no personal interest in your success. They couldn't care less if you prosper or go down the drain. Nor do they have any expertise in strategic planning or marketing. And, to top it off, they are typically ignorant—they don't know what you could offer to add value to their life. So, what do you expect when you simply follow the results of your market research, telling you what consumers think they want from you? Can you really expect to avoid commoditisation? Is blindly doing what consumers ask for really a recipe for revitalising a brand?

Consider the retail banking industry as an example. The scenario looks like this: all the major retail banks invest significant budgets into consumer research. They all do customer satisfaction studies. They all monitor the market to find out what the market wants. And they all attempt to deliver what the market wants. All the mainstream competitors get more or less the same feedback from the market and, in responding to that feedback, move in the same direction. A bit of benchmarking against the other major banks should also ensure that the approach they take in satisfying the stated consumer demands won't vary much between them. And, given that innovation in retail banking is largely based on third-party technology such as internet banking, ATM networks and smart cards, sameness will be maintained in the innovation arena as well.

By leaving it to the market to determine their future vision, the banks are accelerating commoditisation. The banks seem to have forgotten one of the most important tenets in marketing: *don't let the market define your future!*

Having said that, let us now make one point absolutely clear: we are not suggesting that banks should not address customers' concerns, or that they should simply ignore their wants. The point is that by doing so they simply become acceptable. They would only achieve *positive differentiation* if their competitors are hopeless at addressing customers' concerns and preferences — and this is rarely the case.

Notwithstanding what I have said so far, there is one very significant benefit a bank will gain by addressing challenges and opportunities in the same way its competitors are. It will improve its chances of *keeping its customers*, as customers in a commoditised market will usually be lost only when they are dissatisfied, rather than by being spirited away by a competitor.

Think about politics: with a lack of differentiation between the major parties, elections are typically lost rather than won. The same applies to brands. If competitive brands are undifferentiated, decisions will be made on the basis of convenience, price and habit. Unless any of these factors change due to extraneous circumstances (such as moving to an area where 'my' bank does not have a branch close by), customers are likely to stay put, provided they are satisfied with the service. Customer satisfaction is therefore important, because it allows the company to keep its customers, but it is rarely an effective new business development tool.[7]

The most important point is this: *reacting to consumer demands does NOT provide the bank with a powerful vision for the future.*

Does any bank really believe they can build their future around a vision such as: 'We will be the bank that responds most effectively and completely to the demands of our customers'?

It won't work. Why? Customers don't know what is and what is not possible. Their comments are invariably informed by past experiences rather than future possibilities. This is why, when Henry Ford was asked if he undertook market research to inform his development of the motor car, he said, 'If I had asked my customers what they wanted, they would have said a faster horse!'

Did retail banking customers ask for internet banking before they experienced the internet? Did they ask for

---

7   I have to admit that I have oversimplified the matter, as customers are quite likely to shop around when it comes to major purchases such as home loans. However, this does not invalidate my comments regarding the current degree of commoditisation in the retail banking market.

ATMs before they experienced an ATM? In fact, market research conducted before ATMs were introduced showed that the majority of consumers said they would never use a machine for their transactions! Of course, most of them changed their minds once ATMs had been introduced.

The problem is that simply reacting to consumer demands leads to a lack of differentiation and further commoditisation of the category. When all banks simply strive to deliver a more efficient service, then none of them stands out in any way.

WHAT IS MARKETING'S FUTURE?

Having gone through a range of reasons that explain why markets commoditise and why price and convenience dominate many purchase decisions, it may look like strategic marketing has little future. We may as well focus on tactical initiatives only and put the money we save into more price promotions.

... simply reacting to consumer demands leads to a lack of differentiation and further commoditisation of the category.

The truth of the matter is obviously more balanced than such an extreme view. First, I note that in a commoditised market, where consumers tend to buy the same brand habitually, promotions can lead to consumers buying more of a promoted brand and less of other brands in the consideration set, because even something basic like a promotion will stick out when nothing much else differentiates between those brands.[8]

---

8   But keep in mind that Ehrenberg's panel studies have shown that such promotional activities are unlikely to attract consumers who don't already have the promoted brand in their consideration set. This at least holds true for FMCG markets.

Second, the astute marketer will solidify the territory acquired by building barriers to exit in a number of ways. These include loyalty programs, increasing the diversity of customer relationships (for example, selling multiple products to the same customer), and complicated forms that have to be completed when leaving the relationship.

Third, and most importantly, the real marketing challenge is to turn mature brands once again into growth brands, that is, to revitalise mature brands. To do this effectively a company must not only identify and implement a high-impact revitalisation strategy, it must also abolish work practices that neutralise the revitalisation efforts by contributing to commoditisation.

KEY POINTS

- Maturity is typically due to:

  ○ category commoditisation, that is, a lack of meaningful differentiation between competing brands

  ○ a decline in relevance, that is, the benefits the brand offers have lost their appeal or importance.

- Executives often contribute significantly to the commoditisation of their target markets. Typical commoditisation drivers are:

  ○ an obsession with short-term price promotions

  ○ taking a process-driven approach to brand strategy planning

- ○ copying what successful competitors do by relying on benchmarking

- ○ focusing on third-party technologies when innovating

- ○ offering an excessive number of often meaningless features that confuse and/or bore the market

- ○ focusing on simply delivering what the consumer is asking for, that is, delegating strategy development to consumer market research.

CHAPTER 3

ADOPT NEW
WORK PRACTICES

In an ideal world, our goals should determine our strategies, and our strategies should determine our capabilities mix and our work practices. This should then determine the way we organise ourselves, that is, our organisational structure.

In the real world, we find that structure and work practices determine strategy, simply because they impose limitations on what can be done. In other words, an organisation's competencies are influenced significantly by existing structures and work practices, and unless there is a willingness to change these in light of new challenges that demand a fresh approach, there is little hope that a strategy will be implemented as intended.

THE IMPORTANCE OF WORK PRACTICES

Work practices tend to be more significant than the organisational structure in determining the organisation's ability to perform because effective work practices can overcome structural barriers and bridge structural gaps. Inappropriate work practices will hold the organisation back even when the structure is sound.

At the centre of it lies decision making. How the organisation makes decisions determines the speed with which it can move. It determines the purity of the decision, as decisions made by committees or on the basis of trade-offs across units or functions are ineffective compromises. Decision-making processes determine the time frame for any commitments made. For example, decisions that are primarily shaped by short-term pressures are often ineffective in the long term.

... the way decisions are made and enforced in an organisation is the most critical success factor.

Ultimately, the way decisions are made and enforced in an organisation is the most critical success factor. And unless decision making is aligned with the strategic requirements it is not likely that an organisation will be able to implement its revitalisation strategy effectively.

For an executive it may not be obvious that decision making is in fact a work practice. Something we do as part of our daily job rarely is looked at within a broader context. The fact is that decision making and the enforcement of these decisions represent core work practices.

Another key issue relates to the tools we use to prepare the ground for making decisions. For example, if we use outdated and largely ineffective market research tools we are not likely to offer decision makers the in-depth insights and context they need to make a sound decision. In this section I will explore the approach to decision making and some of the tools used to deliver essential inputs to making decisions.

FROM DETERMINISM TO FLEXIBILITY

It is important not to fall into the trap of adopting a strategy as the blueprint that determines what action to take. This may sound odd. Aren't strategies supposed to determine action, that is, be the blueprint for implementing the program we have developed? They are, but only as long as they are the best strategies we can come up with. The problem is that in many organisations the strategy, once completed, replaces thinking. The strategy is implemented blindly, and reward and recognition are based on a manager's success in implementing the strategy rather than their ability to see change and re-evaluate and refocus the strategy as needed.

Leaders of major organisations learned some time ago that a detailed corporate plan is likely to create a barrier to change when the corporation is operating in a rapidly changing environment. The reason is obvious: having 'sold in' the corporate plan with great fanfare, having aligned reward schemes with the achievement of key outcomes defined by that plan, having restructured the organisation to ensure it can effectively implement the plan, and having pinned the corporate leadership and what it stands for to this corporate plan, the plan has been elevated to 'Ten Commandments' status.

The organisation adopts the corporate plan as the yardstick against which to measure progress and success. It is quickly forgotten that this plan describes an abstract, simple world that doesn't really exist, and that as soon as the plan had been completed it would have already been out-of-date.

The same problems occur when a detailed brand revitalisation strategy determines the actions of the marketing and product development departments, the advertising agency and other relevant parties. The brand revitalisation strategy—and its associated planning document—becomes the focus, rather than the real world.

Given that in brand revitalisation we are typically trying to break with the traditional ways of dealing with the brand, we would have to expect some trial and error. This is not to suggest that we need to live through a series of flops before we work out how to get the job done. But early experiences will allow us to adapt our strategy with more impact. Early successes may open up opportunities we did not anticipate. Slow progress may signal a need to refocus or diversify our strategies.

This means that we cannot accept our strategies as predetermining the path we will travel, no matter what. If we do this, we may be lucky and only find that the full potential of the brand is not realised. Or we may be unlucky and find that, due to our obsession with implementing the 'strategy as agreed', we have missed some significant developments in the operating environment that render our strategy ineffective.

But it is not only the risk of missing important opportunities or threats, or not exploiting the brand's full potential. There is also the problem that we need to 'un-sell' the strategy when we want to replace it with a new strategy that is more effective in the changed environment. This process of 'un-selling' takes time and, importantly, staff who have committed totally to a particular strategy will be emotionally frustrated when that strategy is ditched, even if it is replaced by a more effective one.

However, what is likely to have a long life (unless we really got it wrong or experience such a dramatic and unexpected change in market or competitive conditions that our whole thinking has become outdated) is our vision and the associated broad goals that give it substance. Therefore, it is important from the very start to always present the vision as the focal point of what we do—to be guided by *what* we want to achieve, rather than by *how* we will achieve it. The latter will need to *... be guided by* what *we want to achieve, rather than by* how *we will achieve it.* change over time, but the former should be relevant and meaningful for the long term and should provide us with a clear focus whenever the strategy needs to be reconsidered and adapted.

It follows that the revitalisation strategy needs to be kept alive—it needs to grow and adapt, going through a process of evolution that allows the strategy to overcome new challenges and exploit new opportunities as they unfold.

BUILDING THE INGENUITY OF THE ORGANISATION

Differentiation is worth very little unless it is sustainable or renewable. Given the trends and developments outlined in earlier sections, we would expect differentiation in many product categories to rely more heavily on intangible differences. That is, rely more on the brand and what it embodies, than on the tangible differences in the product offer. Furthermore, we believe that the challenge will increasingly be to renew rather than to sustain differentiation. In other words, we have to find new ways of giving meaning to our brand differentiation that is relevant and powerful within a constantly changing environment.

It follows that ingenuity—the ability to find practical solutions to problems—is an asset that will increase in importance as we move forward into a less predictable environment. There are already numerous companies that have started to seriously invest in the development of their organisation's ingenuity. Ingenuity strategies typically have two components: first, the problem-solving skills of *employees* are raised to new heights; second, the problem-solving skills of the *organisation* are lifted.

This often happens initially within the framework of well-defined processes taking place in specific functional areas, such as introducing Six Sigma to repetitive manufacturing processes. Sooner or later, the organisation realises that these processes are great when the objective is to improve repetitive processes. However, they tend to be somewhat limited when it comes to finding *new ways of doing things*. Thus, programs and tools that develop creative or practical problem-solving skills are introduced that can be used for strategic as well as operational problems, solving efficiency as well as effectiveness challenges.

While it is relatively easy for individual managers and staff to improve their ingenuity through the active development of their intuitive and creative problem-solving skills, it is much more difficult to lift the ingenuity of an organisation. The organisation loses its ability to find and implement practical solutions because it gets set in its ways. I don't want to turn this discussion into an elaborate treatise on this matter, which has been well documented elsewhere. But focusing specifically on brand revitalisation strategies, we note the structures, systems and processes that govern how the marketing and/or product development departments work and how they work with outside suppliers, such as communications agencies, are *typically designed to support efficiency and a degree of incremental innovation, but rarely disruptive innovation.*

In other words, they optimise efficiency and support the way things are done now. They make us 'better' at 'doing things the way we do them now'. Doing this actually strengthens the barriers to change. New solutions that require a different mix of skills and perspectives may never be considered, and those that require a change in structures, systems and processes are likely to be rejected.

I note in this context the difficulties major corporations have with diversification based on innovation, as long as the fledgling business venture is kept in-house. The processes, structures and systems that are designed to run a large organisation efficiently kill innovation. After all, innovation typically comes from doing things differently, if not doing different things altogether. Again, this has been well documented elsewhere.

In summary, the organisation needs to develop a high level of ingenuity to be able to continuously renew the differentiation that provides the basis for the brand's success. Developing the ingenuity of employees is a good start, but a review of organisational work practices, identifying those that stifle marketing innovation, is a necessary second step.

FROM TRADITIONAL MARKET RESEARCH TO LEADING-EDGE METHODOLOGIES

One of the first hurdles a revitalisation strategy needs to take is often a consumer concept test. It is natural that decision makers want some market feedback to ensure they are on the right track. But can a concept test really provide reliable feedback? Consider the following:

At least two-thirds of new products fail within the first year of their launch (some statistics put the percentage as high as 90 per cent), yet the vast majority of these products, and their launch campaigns, have been researched with consumers, often using qualitative as well as quantitative methodologies.

There is also ample anecdotal evidence, including these classics:

- the Sony Walkman bombed in research and was only ever launched because Chairman Morita insisted—only to become one of the greatest product successes ever

- the Edsel—allegedly the most researched car concept ever—became one of the most dramatic new product failures ever

- Baileys Irish Cream bombed in group discussions and then went on to become a hugely successful product (and has recently successfully rejuvenated its brand).

Unfortunately, concept testing suffers from very significant limitations. These limitations are generally due to the fact that we are testing only elements of the final product or advertisement, and this test is carried out by using a small sample of consumers in an unnatural setting.

Naturally, there is no point in testing a product or ad once it has been made—it would be too late to discover that it is not likely to realise your objectives. Hundreds of thousands, if not millions of dollars would have been spent already. However, we need to take into account that we are not testing the finished product or ad, but a simple concept board or model, typically used in conjunction with a narrative. We cannot expect this test to give us the same reaction as the finished piece of communication.

... emotions are far more important to memory retention than a rational argument.

Think about advertising concept testing: if our concept boards or animatics were able to generate the same emotional engagement as a finished ad we would never need to produce any ads—we could simply use the concept boards on TV!

The fact that people do not think in words but in images highlights the importance of the sensory input an advertisement provides through its execution. It is also important to note that emotions are far more important to memory retention than a rational argument. In fact, if an idea does not have any emotional significance we are not likely to store it in memory. Again, emotions are often brought alive through execution. A concept board can hardly be expected to create the emotions a finished ad will generate.

Importantly, about 95 per cent of thought, emotion and learning occur in the non-conscious mind. This means we are not consciously aware of these processes and thus can't reliably report them in a research situation. This doesn't render concept testing useless. It means that we have to be sensitive to the fact that we have only tested a concept when we interpret the test results, rather than falling victim to the naive idea that the results are fully representative of the results we may have got had we tested the finished ad. A particular limitation is that many of these concept tests are carried out in group discussions. Focus groups are very effective when the task is to find out about issues such as:

- does the target group understand the concept?

- are there negative or undesirable associations?

- does the concept create strong associations with other brands or products?

- is the intended message understood?

- is the product easy to use?

Clearly, even if only some of the focus group participants don't understand the concept or the message, it is time to adapt or change the concept. It doesn't matter that these participants are *not* representative of the total target group. However, there is no point in asking group participants which ad will be more effective, that is, which will influence their decision 'to buy' more strongly.

There are several very good reasons why we should not ask this question or, at the very least, ignore their answers. First, you have to expect to get a wide range of meaningless rationalisations when you pay eight people to spend 90 minutes analysing a couple of advertising concepts. Have you ever sat down and discussed an advertising concept for an hour and a half? You get on to points that are totally irrelevant, but, hey, you are paid to contribute (and reminded of that by the moderator who is trying to draw everybody into the conversation, even if they have nothing to say), so you do!

Second, participants are influenced by what other participants say. In an experiment, a person was placed into various group discussions held to explore a common topic, unbeknown to the moderator or any of the other participants. At random, this 'mole' got into the discussion early, taking a strongly positive or negative view. It turned out that for more than 80 per cent of the groups attended, the results were in tune with the stance this participant took during the early phases of the group discussion.

Third, there is not enough time to allow for in-depth discussion. As Professor John R Hauser from MIT's Sloan School of Management said, 'If you have two hours to cover five to 10 topics with eight people, then you have about one or two minutes on each topic with each person. You can't possibly get much beyond the surface given those constraints'.

This is what Harvard's Professor Gerald Zaltman, a leading consumer behaviourist, has to say about focus groups: 'Contrary to conventional wisdom, focus groups are not effective when testing ads or evaluating brand images. Nor do they get at deeper thoughts and feelings among consumers. The most disturbing concern about focus groups is that little scientific foundation, from any discipline, supports their use.'[1]

Some research firms have developed a database allowing the researchers to identify the characteristics of successful advertisements, and to track ads that had been concept tested before their launch, thus providing feedback on the accuracy of concept test results. However, what happens when an advertisement is breaking new ground? What happens when it is supposed to change the maps in consumers' minds, the way they make decisions and the way they behave? When it comes to the revitalisation of brands, this should be the norm, not the exception.

Clearly, consumers assess concepts within the reference framework history has equipped them with. Historical data is a useful guide for predicting future behaviour when there are no significant changes in consumers' thinking. However, breakthrough advertising is supposed to change the way consumers think—and the way they make purchase decisions.

---

1   G Zaltman, *How Customers Think: essential insights into the mind of the market*, Harvard Business School Press, 2003.

As Niall Fitzgerald, Chairman Emeritus of Unilever, said, 'Real winners do not play by the rules—they change them or even make their own!' Clearly, when the objective is to change the rules, historical databases will be of less use.

Consider the introduction of the ATM once again. Market research overwhelmingly showed that consumers would not use ATMs. As we all know, these research results were totally misleading. The problem was that consumers were exposed to a new way of thinking and acting that did not align with their existing thought and behavioural patterns. Making financial transactions literally on the street, dealing with a machine, made no sense to them. There was no context, no experience base for them to evaluate this new concept in a realistic way.

Similarly, consumers rejected the Sony Walkman when the concept was researched because the context within which they evaluated the proposition was based on equipment that could play and record music. The early Walkman did not allow for recording—it was a product that changed consumer behaviour with respect to listening occasions, not an incremental advance on traditional tape recorders. Baileys Irish Cream was rejected because the concept of mixing alcohol and cream was new and did not line up with the existing concept of what alcoholic drinks are. Baileys created a new subcategory.

Having said this, the natural question is: how can we improve our ability to make such judgements?

Procter & Gamble, one of the world's most respected and successful marketers, has totally reinvented the way it does business over the last few years. In their book

The Game-Changer, AG Lafley and his co-author, Ram Charan, talk about the many changes that have finally led to P&G becoming an organisation that is driven by innovation.[2] Importantly, they stress how work practices needed to change to achieve this. One of the areas they cover is market research. P&G has been — and still is — totally committed to market research. However, it has just about abandoned group discussions and run-of-the-mill large-scale surveys, instead engaging in immersion programs, observation studies and generally more advanced and insightful techniques.

Here is what Lafley has to say:

> *We invested serious money, resources, time, and management intensity to make our core strengths stronger. For example, we've reinvented our highly valued market research organization and focused it on deep consumer understanding. Our research has moved away from traditional focus group research and invested heavily, to the tune of a billion dollars (double the industry average), in consumer and shopping research, with particular focus on immersive research.*

> *We're spending far more time in context with consumers — living with them in their homes, shopping with them in stores, and being part of their lives. These real-world connections lead to richer consumer insights, faster speed to market, and lower risks. It alters the mind-set of P&G leaders and changes their decision making.*

> *… This total immersion leads to richer consumer insights, which helps identify innovation opportunities that are often missed by traditional research.[3]*

---

2   AG Lafley & R Charan, *The Game-changer: how you can drive revenue and profit growth with innovation*, Crown/Random House, 2008, p. 13.

3   Lafley & Charon, p. 47.

The point I made earlier applies here as well: to successfully implement new strategies often requires a change in established work practices. If management is not committed to such a change then the strategy won't be implemented effectively and, as a result, the hoped for (if not outright expected) results won't be delivered.

CHAPTER 4

MOVE FROM EXPERT TO INTUITIVE STRATEGY

The challenges facing senior executives who determine the corporation's future by deciding on strategies have changed significantly over the last decade.

Given the complexity of markets and the unpredictability of competitive moves there has always been a degree of uncertainty to contend with. However, there seems to be general agreement that today we are experiencing a deadly combination of uncertainty, complexity and accelerated change in the operating environment.

But while the environment within which we have to make decisions has changed significantly, we seem to be stuck with processes, systems and structures that were developed for an environment that allowed us to place more value on predicting the future than on dealing with unforeseen operating conditions. Important strategic decision-making processes are largely carried out at our leisure. That is, we fit them into some regular planning cycle that suits us rather than reflects the environment we are operating in. Clearly, companies tend to value the gathering and analysis of historical data far more than the speed with which decisions are made.

... companies tend to value the gathering and analysis of historical data far more than the speed with which decisions are made.

In an environment where history is a sound guide to the future this, of course, makes sense. But what of an environment that changes rapidly, where strategies that worked in the past are quickly outdated? Our decision-making processes are typically not designed for such an environment.

This doesn't mean that management simply ignores change. Rather, managers are spending more of their valuable time managing crises—crises that could have been avoided had the approach to decision making been designed for a fluid rather than a reasonably stable environment.

This book is not about management as such, but specifically about the revitalisation of mature brands. The broad observations made above may therefore seem to be out of context. However, there is an important point to be made: it is possible to revitalise a mature brand by moving faster.

The ability to capitalise on opportunities and to manage changed conditions that nobody could foresee faster than anyone else provides a company with a competitive advantage. Similarly, marketing's ability to adapt a brand strategy quickly and effectively provides the brand with a competitive advantage. In the case of a mature brand, it may well be the key ingredient of a revitalisation strategy.

THE PROBLEM: THE FUTURE LOOKS LESS LIKE THE PAST

Our improved understanding of how the brain works has allowed us to also gain deeper insights into how we make decisions. The result is that, today, we know there are two very different paths that can be taken when making a decision.

Let's start with our expert mind. Our brain stores constructs or patterns which represent memories. When we are facing a new situation, our brain compares the new situation with past memory patterns to see if there are any matches that could inform our decision. Gary Klein[1] is the expert who has allowed us to learn about such decision-making processes. Over many years he and his team have worked with people who have to make decisions on the spot, such as firefighters, hospital emergency personnel, tank drivers, jet fighters and ambulance crews. They don't have time to analyse situations at great length, or to ponder the impact of alternative decisions. In fact, if they don't decide immediately, somebody might die — and it may even be themselves.

When Klein started his work, he assumed that these decisions would be made on the basis of a quick, analytical evaluation of alternative courses of action. He found that this early hypothesis was wrong. Rather, a new situation

---

1   G Klein, *Sources of Power: how people make decisions*, MIT Press, 1999.

is compared with existing memory patterns and, as soon as a memory pattern 'fits', showing a viable strategy that worked in the past, this strategy is adopted. Only when this strategy turns out not to work, will the expert's brain conduct another search through memory patterns to find an alternative strategy.

While we don't have the same urgency to make decisions on the spot in the world of management, it seems that this approach comes to us naturally. Our brain is designed to compare existing memory patterns with a new situation and to very quickly identify any (partial) matches. In fact, our brain's capacity to do this is unsurpassed by any supercomputer. It is not likely that we will be able to develop a computer that can match, let alone exceed, our brain's capacity when it comes to matching complex patterns comprised of sensory inputs and emotions.

We value experience as expressed by the learning curve, a graph that shows how we become better at doing something when we do it more often. And, in many situations where we repeat activities, moving up the learning curve is in fact the key ingredient to success.

Given all this, it won't come as a surprise that the natural approach to making management decisions is to rely on past experience, that is, to compare a new situation with relevant memory patterns. We may not do this in a conscious, planned way. Rather, our brain will automatically go through the process of comparing memory patterns and deliver us an 'expert opinion' should we have dealt with similar patterns before.

Without doubt there are numerous issues in an organisation where disruptive change is not required, and may not even be desirable. An approach that relies on historical memory patterns serves us well in these instances. However, the rejuvenation of brands requires, by definition, a fresh approach. Resorting naturally to what worked in the past may severely limit our ability to identify and implement an innovative strategy.

Stated differently: *in an environment where change is the order of the day and where we need fresh strategies to break out of commoditisation and convince the consumer that we have something worthwhile to offer, there is little benefit in being very good at doing what we have always done.*

EXPERT AND INTUITIVE
BATTLE STRATEGIES

William Duggan[2] wrote an excellent book on expert and intuitive strategy. He suggests that expert strategy is very much based on the scientific method:

1. develop a hypothesis

2. test the hypothesis

3. validate or falsify the hypothesis

4. start again ...

However, while our culture supports this approach and accepts it as being a rational way of making decisions,

---

2   W Duggan, *Strategic Intuition: the creative spark in human achievement*, Columbia Business School Publishing, 2007.

Duggan points out that breakthrough, disruptive innovations are usually not based on the scientific approach. From the discovery of the atom and medical breakthroughs such as penicillin, to disruptive business models including Google and Microsoft, Duggan demonstrates that it was in fact intuitive rather than expert thinking that was at play.

Intuitive strategy is also based on patterns, but rather than simply selecting memory patterns that fit, we need to create new patterns that represent a dramatically different perspective of the challenge we are facing. This allows us to see new strategic options. In other words, expert strategy relies on *pattern recognition*, while intuitive strategy relies on *pattern making*.

Duggan presents an interesting point taken from the *Art of War*. More specifically, he compares the approach advocated by Baron Antoine Jomini, who became the father of modern warfare, with that of Von Clausewitz. Jomini suggested you win a battle when you have greater force than your enemy at the *objective* point, that is, the point that has traditionally been identified as being critical to success. In other words, past battles may have been won because a strategically placed city or landmark was captured. Thus, in a new battle we identify which city or landmark is in a central position and then focus our total efforts on capturing it.

... you have to identify a decisive point where you can win ...

Von Clausewitz, on the other hand, believes that we should not try to identify an objective point, which is simply applying conventional thinking to a new challenge. Rather, he advocates that we should seek the *decisive* point — the point where we believe we can win the battle, regardless of where it may be or what conditions it may be fought under.

For example, when Napoleon invaded Italy from the north, he was expected to focus on capturing the major cities of northern Italy. However, Napoleon felt that he could not win the war there and simply went past these cities. The Italians were dumbfounded, as this was totally out of line with conventional warfare. In the end they decided to attack and chased after Napoleon, who defeated them in a series of battles in strategically unimportant places.

The important point is that Napoleon did not decide a priori that he would capture a particular city or fight the battle in a particular place. He engaged when he believed he had spotted a decisive point, where he could actually win the battle, rather than following the wisdom of conventional warfare.

In summary, Jomini believed you must have greater force than your enemy at the objective point, that is, the point where convention suggests battles are won or lost. Von Clausewitz believes you have to identify a decisive point where you can win, rather than follow conventional warfare which is based on historical facts.

EXPERT OR INTUITIVE STRATEGY TO REVITALISE YOUR BRAND?

Let's now apply these key principles to the revitalisation of mature brands. For argument's sake, let us assume we are dealing with an FMCG brand. In the category under consideration we find that, in the past, advertising expenditure correlated with success. In other words, brands that consistently outspent their competitors tended to gain additional market share points as a result.

Baron Jomini would advocate a massive advertising campaign. The rules of warfare, he would suggest, show that you have to outspend your competitor to win the battle. You have to bring superior force to play (a larger advertising budget) at the objective point (where consumers are exposed to advertising). I might add that it would not just be a matter of having a bigger budget, but you would have to match or better your competitors with respect to media choice and be creative as well, that is, create more effective advertising touchpoints.

... in the development of intuitive strategy you draw together selected elements from different situations to create new combinations.

If, on the other hand, you take Von Clausewitz's advice, you would not automatically go down this road. You may in fact decide that you can't outspend your competitors. But while this would be a problem if you were a student of Baron Jomini, Von Clausewitz would not consider this a show-stopper. He would encourage you to use your intuition to find a *decisive* point—a point where you *can* win—rather than simply accept convention and play by the old rules.

The essential difference is that when developing expert strategy you are looking for history to tell you what worked in similar situations in the past, while in the development of intuitive strategy you draw together selected elements from different situations to create new combinations.

At this stage executives tend to get a bit nervous. Expert strategy can be easily sold. After all, it builds on facts. We know what worked in the past and we use this knowledge to win again. Dealing with 'known knowns' provides a feeling of comfort. It is not threatening. After all, we have been trained in making 'expert' decisions based on our past memory patterns since childhood, so we feel comfortable with this approach.

Intuitive strategy, on the other hand, is more of a search process. We can't even debate the merits of our strategy at the outset, because the whole point is that we are seeking to identify our decisive point rather than focusing on the objective point.

Consider two consultants. One presents a historical overview of how FMCG brands have managed to out-perform their competitors. Data shows that brands that outspent their competitors tended to win market share points. The consultant recommends a massive advertising campaign.

The other consultant suggests that the market and comp-etitive environment have changed and fresh solutions are required to win. She also points out that a massive advertising campaign may well allow the company to capture some market share points, but that such spending is unsustainable and thus success is likely to be short-lived. The answer, the consultant assures, lies in finding new ways of competing — in breaking industry conventions.

Which consultant is likely to win the assignment? The consultant who presents a conventional, well-understood approach that lines up with management's own experiences (memory patterns)? Or the consultant who does not actually present a firm strategy at all, but asserts that some funds need to be spent to work out how to break industry convention, to find a decisive point where the battle can be won in a decisive manner?

Most executives would appoint the first consultant. I hope you wouldn't, because if you are serious about revitalising your mature brand you are most likely in need of a strategy that breaks convention. In fact, I would go so far as to suggest that if conventional thinking were all that was needed you would not have a mature brand, because you would already have revitalised it.

The challenge most custodians of mature brands face is that conventional approaches don't work any longer. The operating environment has changed. Maybe commoditisation in your category is much more advanced than ever before. Maybe consumers have become indifferent to your brand. Maybe product innovation that worked in the past has lost its edge. There could be many reasons, but whatever they are, they are likely to point towards the need for fresh thinking, for a strategy that breaks industry conventions.

HOW CAN WE STRENGTHEN OUR INTUITIVE DECISION MAKING?

As is typically the case when we talk about changing or improving the way we think, we can either resort to tools or we can train our mind. The essential task is to create rich, new patterns by making new connections.

The tools we use are typically called 'creative techniques'. Most of these, including lateral thinking, are based on the principle that we need to make new connections. This means developing new patterns which we would not have come across by simply reviewing our brain's memory bank. When we use brainstorming we give ourselves permission to make new connections, recognising that many of these will be quite useless, but we may find a highly unusual and effective solution among the mountain of useless ideas.

Advanced techniques such as morphological box analysis ask us to first create combinations of factors using an analytical approach, applying brainstorming to these new combinations. This helps ensure that we leave conventional thinking and delve even deeper into a new world.

Much has been written about creative techniques and I won't even attempt to summarise it here. However, a few words of caution are in order:

- The use of creative techniques is not likely to lead to a new, effective solution quickly. If it were that easy, none of us would be working. We would all have worked out some amazing get-rich scheme and be lying in the sun on the beach of our own personal tropical island.

- In my experience, few companies use brainstorming effectively. Getting together to throw around some ideas is not brainstorming. You have to follow the brainstorming rules if you want to get anywhere.

- Companies such as Ideo that use brainstorming regularly and with great success typically don't use a basic brainstorming technique. There are a multitude of advanced techniques that can be applied. The challenge is to find the right creative technique for the task at hand and to establish a creative group internally that gets used to working with these techniques.

I have already mentioned that an alternative to using tools is to 'train the brain' to make fresh connections (these are not mutually exclusive options). Again, this is not particularly difficult. Our brain is designed to accommodate learning. In fact, it will allocate additional neurons to tasks we carry out frequently. All we have to do is to be persistent when it comes to exercising our brain.

First, we may want to improve the mind's intuitive pattern-making capabilities by ensuring ongoing input of new patterns through engaging in new experiences. Just think about it this way: who is more likely to generate new connections and thus come up with new ways of addressing a challenge: a person who does the same things every day, or a person who frequently exposes themselves to new sensory inputs?

A very simple approach is to 'feed' your brain new experiences by doing the unusual. Go and see a movie you would not normally have chosen. Find a new way to go to work or home after work. Read a section of the newspaper you would not normally read. Play a game you have never played before, and so on. Exposing yourself to new experiences creates a host of new memory patterns that can be used to create new, unconventional ones.

This is a huge topic in its own right and I am merely scratching the surface here. From the strategy point of view

I note that if you rely on expert strategy (that is, if you let yourself be guided by past experiences), you will most likely end up with a fairly conventional revitalisation strategy. In fact, there is every chance that even if you start out with a disruptive, fresh strategy, you will—step by step—adjust it to bring it back to something more conventional, simply because you will feel more comfortable with something that can be validated by past experience.

If you do want to break out of the rut of commoditisation and truly revitalise your brand, you will have to consider an intuitive strategy. Spend time to search for the decisive point rather than simply accept industry convention. Do allow for the exploration of the unlikely and unusual. Too often we accept that creative solutions are the domain of creative staff in advertising agencies, while the strategy needs to be rational and based on facts (historical data). We need to drop this assumption—it is untenable in a rapidly changing operating environment.

... to make an impact we need a strategy ... that breaks out of conventional thinking and accepts the risk inherent in taking a new path ...

If we want to make an impact we need a strategy that is creative—or intuitive, as Duggan would call it—that breaks out of conventional thinking and accepts the risk inherent in taking a new path we haven't travelled before. The risk is balanced by the opportunity of creating history by revitalising a mature brand that has been all but written off. The key is to find the decisive point rather than to accept the objective point that is based on industry convention. Some of the strategic options explored in this book may help you to find this point. But at the end of the day it will be your mindset above all that will determine which strategy you will adopt.

KEY POINTS

- Today's decision-making environment is characterised by a deadly combination of uncertainty, complexity and accelerated change.

- Rapid and unpredictable changes in the operating environment render long-term planning ineffective.

- The emphasis has to shift from lengthy planning cycles that assume a reasonably predictable environment to a flexible approach, characterised by fast decision making.

- It is important to note that I am not advocating reactive management. Rather, a clear brand vision and clear objectives ensure that decisions are consistently moving the brand in the desired direction.

- Most executives subscribe to 'expert strategy', an approach to strategy development that is historically based and assumes that the brand's battle strategy can be pre-planned on the basis of past experience.

- However, 'intuitive strategy', an approach where the outcome is well defined, but the strategy is developed and adapted as events unfold, is more effective in markets and industries where change is unpredictable and sometimes rapid.

- There are tools and exercises we can use to strengthen our intuitive thinking capabilities. These can be useful and powerful, but the most important first step is for the executive to adopt intuitive strategy as an approach whenever the decision-making environment suggests that historically based approaches are unlikely to be effective.

PART II

REVITALISATION STRATEGIES

The day we believe there are rules we can follow to revitalise a brand is the day we abandon the creativity and insightfulness required to succeed at this challenge. Recognising that every case is different, there are some general guidelines that are likely to be of use (not always, but quite often). The following pages provide an overview on what I consider to be some of the most important pointers as you embark on the road of awakening your giant.

The elephant grid can be a useful tool for a reality check. It suggests that much of what we do may be necessary but not sufficient to gain a positive differentiation. We have to invest in such strategies because they ensure that the brand is acceptable—a possible choice. But they don't position the brand in a meaningful, high-impact way, allowing it to gain a leadership position which will be reflected in market share growth.

In the elephant grid we refer to these positions as the 'herd' and the 'bull' elephant positions, respectively. It is a good idea when considering revitalisation strategies to think back to this grid and ask if the strategy under consideration would truly give your brand a bull elephant position in the marketplace.

Figure 5.1: the elephant grid

High	**Herd elephant:** One of several brands that satisfies the market's requirements. It's in the race, but there is no reason for it to win.	**Bull elephant:** A brand that is strongly differentiated in a meaningful and important way—it delights the market.
	White elephant: A meaningless, but not offensive, differentiation. Precious resources are squandered developing and promoting white elephant features.	**Elephant man:** Really different, but nobody loves you. Standing out in a negative, rather than positive, way.
Low		

RELEVANCE

Low   **DIFFERENTIATION**   High

There are always myriad options that could be investigated or pursued. Every business is different, every brand faces its unique challenges and, while there are some all-encompassing meta-trends, every industry has its own dynamics. It is therefore impossible to present a small set of specific, mutually exclusive strategies to choose from. Rather, the executive has to combine relevant strategic options in a meaningful way, allowing her to address the particular challenges she is facing with respect to the brands in her custody.

The options I present range from searching for delights to the use of brand vision archetypes. I consider whether—and how—the rules of competition could be changed, and explore how the use of symbolism may allow you to highlight the particular competence or advantage your brand offers. I propose that a spirit relationship is essential to the rejuvenation of a brand and suggest that a move from exposure to engagement may allow the brand to build a stronger relationship with the consumer. Sometimes the most effective strategy lies at the master-brand level. Creating a total brand experience is another option covered.

I have tried to stay away from broad-brush recommend-ations such as 'differentiate', 'reposition your brand', 'change your target group' or 'innovate', as such general propositions are not really helpful. Of course, you might have to do one or all of these, but how? At the same time I have to accept that some of the guidelines I am offering are general in nature, as they affect the way you think about the revitalisation challenge rather than offering a specific potential solution. Hopefully, I have got the balance right between presenting specific, narrowly focused options and others that change the way you think and operate as a precursor to finding new insights and directions.

Finally, I note that one of the key challenges you will be facing is to find the right balance between opportunism and self-determination. There is no doubt that the operating environment is changing in unpredictable ways and within unpredictable time frames. It therefore doesn't make sense to simply work out what to do and to then stick with this strategic direction or plan regardless of what's happening around you. At the same time it is unlikely that a business that simply reacts to opportunities and threats, without any strategic direction of its own, will succeed.

CHAPTER 5

DELIVER DELIGHTS

If we are lucky, the maturity of the brand is based on misperceptions. The consumer, inundated with competitive products that claim new features or capabilities, may have developed the perception that our well-established brand has fallen behind. If this is the case, we have obviously failed to communicate, but that can be rectified. After all, we understand the specific deficiencies the consumer associates with our brand and we can deliver tangible evidence that we don't have these deficiencies.

Even then, it is difficult to get a consumer who has become indifferent to our brand to listen. In fact, dealing with indifference is arguably a much greater challenge than dealing with negative perceptions. Consumers with negative perceptions may be hard to convince otherwise, but at least they are listening! Indifferent consumers are not likely to even do us the courtesy of listening to what we have to say.

What we need is nothing short of a delight that surprises and engages. It is quite likely that the mature brand delivered a 'delight' that fuelled its growth at some stage in the past. The problem with delights is that they quickly drift into oblivion. A delight quickly becomes a 'want' and, sooner or later, a 'need'. We first saw this concept applied by Japanese companies. It is a simple, yet powerful way of thinking about what brands are all about.

This concept reminds us that there is a continuous drift from delights to wants and then needs. Thus, when we introduce an innovative new benefit, we hopefully create a delight. The consumer will think or say, 'This is amazing. I have never seen anything like that before! This really makes a difference!' Think of the reaction of safety-conscious drivers when airbags were introduced, or of couch potatoes when remote controls delivered them control over their TV viewing without effort.

However, over time (and usually it doesn't take long) competitors copy the feature and it will become a want. The consumer now says, 'This is a valuable feature. I want a product that offers this feature'. Airbags have advanced at least to 'wants'.

But it does not stop there. Wants tend to eventually become needs and consumers expect any product or service offer to address these needs. While the consumer is actively selecting a product or service that will satisfy a want, they often will not even think about needs as they are assumed to be catered for anyway. For example, we would suggest that remote controls are just basic 'needs' today. When buying a TV one would just expect to get a remote control.

You can see the same stages of development with respect to kettles that automatically switch off when they have boiled; the consumer's right to exchange products the day after they were bought; having an ensuite bathroom in a hotel room; or getting clear sound from even an inexpensive radio or sound system. Or think of mobile phones that can send

... without keeping the delights coming, the brand will mature. It will lose its energy and its differentiation.

SMS messages or car tyres that rarely ever puncture. And what about computers with ports for internet cables, or supermarkets that offer a wide range of leading brands?

This is what life is all about: we get excited and really appreciate the innovative new feature that adds value to our life; next thing, we eliminate brands that don't offer this feature from further consideration; finally, we simply expect that brands offer this feature.

Essentially this means that without keeping the delights coming, the brand will mature. It will lose its energy and its differentiation.

But where do the delights come from? Efforts to identify delights through market research are rarely successful. The reason is that consumers are neither particularly creative, nor do they understand how advances in technology or other relevant areas could be used to develop and deliver delights.

Market research can really only assess wants, but delivering the 'wants' will simply provide the brand with a place in the 'herd'. It will be one of the acceptable options, but delivering the wants will not differentiate the brand and provide it with a competitive advantage.

However, while market research is not likely to identify specific delights, it can help us understand the consumer. Once we understand the consumer and the context within which they use the types of products and services we offer, we should be able to identify delights.

Procter & Gamble has dramatically changed its use of market research methodologies to achieve this. Rather than asking consumers in group discussions or surveys, it conducts immersive research and includes executives in this research. P&G managers routinely spend time with consumers—in their homes, going shopping, when they use relevant products or services. This allows executives to gain an intuitive understanding of the consumer and the challenges the consumer is facing, which in turn allows the company to come up with delights.[1]

... while market research is not likely to identify specific delights, it can help us understand the consumer.

Consensus mapping, developed under Professor Gerald Zaltman's guidance at Harvard Business School's Mind of the Market Laboratory, is an example of a methodology that allows us to gain much deeper insights into how consumers feel about brands, products and relevant spheres of their life.[2] Perhaps not surprisingly, Procter & Gamble can be found among the nine major corporations that have supported the development of this excellent research tool.

1   AG Lafley & R Charan, *The Game-changer: how you can drive revenue and profit growth with innovation*, Crown/Random House, 2008.

2   G Zaltman, *How Customers Think: essential insights into the mind of the market*, Harvard Business School Press, 2003.

Consensus mapping relies much more on images than traditional methodologies. It does not use images as a patch to give the feeling of innovation to an outdated methodology, such as asking group discussion participants to bring a picture or item to the session. Rather, images are used extensively in face-to-face interviews to explore relevant constructs in consumers' minds. A consensus map provides a great platform for the development of delights.

A much earlier methodology that has some timelessness about it is problem detection, which is based on a key principle that had been all but ignored until some smart researcher in a BBDO office developed this methodology. The key principle is that you should not expect the consumer to deliver solutions, but you can expect the consumer to tell you all about their problems—real or perceived.

Consumers can tell us how frequently each problem occurs, how important they are, and how effectively any solutions on offer address them. The resulting priority list guides the development of solutions that delight the consumer. I note in passing that, in many instances, problem detection can also serve as a useful bridge between marketing and R&D because it links market opportunities (problems) with solutions (which may be R&D driven).

In any case, our main point is that last century's problem detection, this century's consensus mapping, and the immersion projects P&G is undertaking are all applied with the same objective in mind: to understand the consumer.

Once we have gained a sound understanding that is not just analytical but intuitive in nature we—the custodians of the brand—can identify solutions. But never delegate the strategy development process to the consumer. Never fall for the researcher making strategic recommendations solely on the basis of what consumers say. The consumer does not know and does not care about your strategy. If you are the brand's custodian, it is you who has to develop the strategy. This is what you get paid for.

And if all this seems pretty obvious, it is amazing how many executives still expect consumer research to deliver the answer to their brand revitalisation challenge.

KEY POINTS

- Consumers rarely make active purchase decisions. Most of their buying is habitual.

- To generate brand loyalty we need to engage the consumer emotionally.

- With a mature brand this invariably means that we need to offer a delight that surprises and engages the consumer. Consumers feel indifferent towards many mature brands, even those they still habitually buy. To break through this wall of indifference and engage we have to surprise and delight.

- It is advisable to apply more advanced research methodologies than traditional group discussions or surveys. We can't expect consumers to tell us what would delight them (in fact, we would hardly surprise them by simply offering what they already know they want).

- Research needs to help us gain a deeper insight into the challenges consumers face and the contexts within which our brand lives or is consumed. It is then the marketer's responsibility to develop delights that will rejuvenate the brand.

CHAPTER 6

THROW YOUR MASTER BRAND INTO BATTLE

This section is only relevant to the custodians of master brands. First question: what's a master brand? As there don't seem to be generally accepted definitions for primary and master brand, let us agree on the definition we will be using here.

PRIMARY BRAND

Typically a corporate brand that is used extensively, if not exclusively, at the product level—usually with additional explanatory or descriptive name components that provide some clarity about the product offer. Examples include a number of leading motor vehicle brands (BMW, Mercedes, Renault) and the electronics industry (Samsung, LG).

Obviously, the primary brand is inextricably linked to the product range. An outdated product range will make it very difficult to revitalise the primary brand but, unfortunately, a mature primary brand towards which consumers feel indifferent will limit the impact of new product launches, even when these products stand up well in a competitive context.

MASTER BRAND

Typically a corporate brand that is kept in the background, endorsing product brands that are the focus of brand promotion and positioning strategies. Examples include Sony (Sony PlayStation, Sony Bravo, Sony VAIO) and General Motors (Chevrolet, Dodge, Hummer).

One of the reasons that master brands have traditionally been kept in the background is that many major corporations have collected strong product brands (and sometimes primary or master brands) through acquisitions. They did not want to weaken the market position of these brands by diluting existing brand equity and thus only hesitatingly applied their own master brand.

This has led to consumers valuing the product brand rather than the master brand. This doesn't mean that the master brand is useless, however; it may still serve as a credibility factor when launching new product brands or products, or when the consumer is considering a trial purchase.

As many corporations have grown through acquisitions, we can quite often find a mix of primary and master brands. For example, Kraft has strong product brands (such as Philadelphia and Vegemite) where the Kraft brand simply endorses the product brand while it uses the Kraft brand as a primary brand on much of its cheese range. In some instances Kraft is not visible at all, as is the case with Toblerone.

In this section we will be focusing on strategies for master brands. When it comes to the revitalisation of brands, master brands can sometimes become a key driver rather than just hover in the background as an insurance policy. To become a driver we need the master brand to develop a strong relationship with the consumer. This invariably means a spirit relationship, and a prerequisite for this is to develop a meaningful role for the master brand.

Figure 6.1: from trust mark to revitalisation driver

From	To
Master brand as a trust mark	**Master brand as the revitalisation driver**
Type of relationship Has been around forever — familiarity = trust.	*Type of relationship* Emotional — what the master brand stands for is relevant, meaningful and engaging
Typical brand vision archetype Guardian = predictable, controlled, i.e. reliable, with no surprises, but also a brand that has no soul.	*Brand vision archetype* Depends on type of relationship but most likely a brand vision archetype with strong emotion
Key benefit Presence of the master brand reduces the risk of purchase.	*Key benefit* The master brand offers intangible benefits that are important to me (e.g. shared values; excitement; help in addressing a key issue or getting something right; etc.)

You may well wonder why we have given the master brand special treatment, given that many of the relevant concepts are the same. The reason is that a master brand that presides over a significant product portfolio and/or has a highly credible market standing has an unprecedented opportunity to engage the consumer in meta-themes.

For a product brand that offers only a limited range of, say, food products, it is usually very difficult to engage the consumer in broadly based, food-related themes. However, the master brand that represents a wide portfolio of products (and product brands) has the legitimacy to engage and to appropriate such territory in the consumer's mind.

For example, it would make sense for Nestlé or Kraft to engage consumers in a nutrition, health, wellbeing, wellness or similar theme, but it would not make much sense for Peters Ice Cream (a Nestlé brand), Kraft Cheese slices or a narrowly based primary brand such as Lindt that stands only for chocolate.

As major diversified companies get more sophisticated in their marketing, we can expect to see them competing for a much bigger share of the emotional relationships consumers are prepared to enter into. It may be far-fetched today to suggest that some brands will truly become life partners, but we believe this will happen within the next 10 years and the foundations are being put in place right now.

The catalyst is often the digital environment that allows a brand to engage the consumer and, by doing so, to add value to the consumer's life. We may not be able to go beyond some emotional appeal with a master brand TV ad, but we can go a lot further online. Here are three examples:

- *Johnson & Johnson's* Caregiver Initiative <www.strengthforcaring.com> offers advice and support on a wide range of topics, from stress relief and finding an appropriate work/life balance, to grief, death and dying, food, fitness and wellness. This microsite offers not only articles and contributions by recognised authorities, but also allows site visitors to comment, tell their stories, ask questions and interact.

- *Mattel* has a microsite <www.webelieveingirls.com> that offers a wide range of articles, hints and tips for raising girls, including activities that parents can take part in with their daughters and an agony aunt-type Q&A section allowing concerned parents to ask for advice. However, we note the lack of branding (undoubtedly intentional) that somewhat limits the transfer to the master brand of the positive emotion this site generates. Most likely it was felt that the brand should be low-key to ensure the site is not seen as primarily a marketing tool, but as an honest means of adding value to parents'—and their daughters'—lives. But would it not have been even better to build the master brand into a brand that stands for such qualities rather than dissociate it from a truly worthwhile effort?

- *Diageo* offers extensive information and guidance related to drinking on its microsite <www.drinkIQ.com>, addressing health, work and relationship issues. Again, information and advice offered is extensive, even though this site offers less opportunity to interact beyond the completion of questionnaires.

There are many more master brands that offer sites that attempt to address consumers' concerns and interests rather than market products and services.

Today, these initiatives are typically implemented at arm's length. That is, rather than the master brand developing a close relationship with the consumer by adding value in a relevant, meaningful and important way, we see the master brand endorsing a separate microsite—often done in a very low-key way.

We believe that the future belongs to master brands that take a strong position rather than a background role. Consumers are likely to adopt a small number of key brands that offer meaningful relationships. Master brands that establish these relationships early are likely to benefit from increased consumer loyalty.

We would expect consumers to initially search using a number of sources when they seek answers to important questions that reflect their deepest concerns and insecurities. Eventually, they are likely to settle on a particular site—and thus brand—that they feel offers the most relevant and reliable information, or allows them to investigate

... the future belongs to master brands that take a strong position rather than a background role.

the specific personal issues that are close to their hearts. Once they have developed a loyal relationship with such a brand, they are not likely to switch to another. Rather, this brand will become their trusted and valued partner as they move through a particular life-cycle phase, or even through life.

As I have already mentioned, I am expressing a view here rather than referring to a validated practice. I feel it makes good sense to expect consumers to establish close, loyal relationships with brands that offer meaningful, even personalised advice and guidance in matters that are of great importance to the consumer. If I am right, we will eventually find a small number of master brands that have exploited this opportunity in commanding positions. It will take several years for such a strategy to pay off, but the return on such an investment could be significant.

If I had to select a brand that has made significant progress in this direction, I would single out *Nestlé*. On its website, Nestlé states, 'Nestlé is the world's foremost Nutrition, Health and Wellness company. We are committed to increasing the nutritional value of our products while improving the taste'. Arguably, Nestlé has acted on its stated values more than most corporations. It has literally spent billions of dollars on aligning existing product groups with its stated values, and on acquisitions that are transforming Nestlé in a step-wise way into a nutrition, health and wellness company.

Nestlé has prepared a very strong foundation that will provide it with a competitive advantage when it comes to giving credibility to its values statement. So far, Nestlé has done little to establish its master brand in an explicit, proud and confident way as the world's foremost nutrition, health and wellness company with consumers. But at the same time, Nestlé has laid the foundation for a major revitalisation of its master brand and could well take its brand into a 'life partner' position. In fact, if Nestlé gets it right—and there is no reason to believe it won't—it might well emerge as the first true *life partner* brand.

Key points

- Master brands can potentially lead the revitalisation effort, with a positive impact across the whole brand portfolio.

- In the long term we see the emergence of life partner brands. These are brands that develop a strong spirit relationship with consumers and maintain their relevance during the consumer's lifetime; a whole-of-life relationship, so to speak.

- To achieve this, a brand needs to have a potentially meaningful role as expressed by the product range it offers. However, while this is typically a prerequisite, it is not sufficient to becoming a life partner brand. The brand also must be seen to add value to the consumer's life by providing guidance and support that is highly valued by consumers.

Chapter 7

Brand vision archetypes[1]

Traditionally, the vision for a brand was derived and talked about in a rational, analytical way. Attributes that were supposed to characterise the brand and define what it stands for were used to communicate the brand to those who needed to understand it: the planners who defined the brand strategy; the marketing executives who made the decisions; and the creative people in the advertising agency who, hopefully, translated these dry descriptions into emotionally powerful communication.

Even the consumer was supposed to understand these analytical descriptions, with much market research based on rating brands against these descriptors, and the communications quite often attempting to directly portray

---

1   See P Steidl, *Survive, Exploit, Disrupt: action guidelines for marketing in a recession*, John Wiley & Sons Australia, 2009, for a more comprehensive discussion on brand vision archetypes.

a particular quality deemed to be characteristic of the brand.

There are three problems with this approach:

- First, it diminishes differentiation. Too many brands are seeking to portray and stand for the same abstract qualities, such as being innovative, consumer friendly, welcoming, grounded, making life easy, exciting, and so forth.

- Second, much gets lost in the translation. Attributes such as welcoming, grounded or exciting mean different things to different people — and even to the same person at different times, depending on the context and prevailing mood.

- Third, the human mind thinks holistically. We *experience* a brand in its totality (if at all), not as a set of particular abstract attributes.

Fortunately, these problems can be resolved through the use of archetypes.

WHO THE BRAND WANTS TO BE KNOWN AS

The issue is not what a brand could do or might do; the question is *who* we want it to be known as. By selecting a particular archetype and living this archetype, the brand will be understood as that archetype. There will be clarity and consumers will be able to develop a meaningful relationship with the brand, because they know who it is.

We all intuitively recognise the same archetypes. This makes archetypes a universal language that is neither segment- nor culture-specific. Importantly, archetypes not only embody certain qualities, but we seem to understand them in a holistic, intuitive way. In other words, we 'know' how a particular archetype would behave in a certain situation, what an archetype would think about an issue, or what values an archetype represents. This makes archetypes an extremely powerful tool when we develop a vision for our brand.

Clearly, many brands do not represent archetypes. They have fuzzy images, because they have not 'lived' a particular archetype. They have a confused personality and their values and actions are not well understood. By using brand vision archetypes we can introduce some meaning into the equation. Consumers start to understand the brand, providing the basis for a relationship to develop. By choosing the right brand vision archetype we not only introduce meaning, but make the brand relevant to its target group. Our target group can relate to the brand and starts to engage with it.

An important point to keep in mind is that archetypes are not stereotypes. The latter are transient—they represent a type of person that may be typical in a particular context and time. Archetypes are permanently ingrained in our thinking, across time and cultures. Archetypes do work. They can help us to understand where a brand is coming from, what it stands for today, and what its future potential might be. The latter is especially important, as it allows us to develop a vision for the brand that can inform our strategies.

Finally, we need to stress that the choice of a brand vision archetype is a choice the custodians of the brand have to make. Market research can tell us if consumers believe a brand represents a particular archetype, but they can't identify the most appropriate vision archetype for the brand. As the term suggests, the challenge is to find an archetype that embodies the brand vision. The single most important factor is the company's ability to bring the chosen brand vision archetype alive. Choosing a brand vision archetype — typically done in a workshop environment — is the easy part. But finding effective ways of bringing this archetype alive is the challenge that must be addressed effectively. If it can't, then the choice is unacceptable and a different archetype needs to be chosen. This is why I spend far more time in brand archetype workshops exploring how preferred archetypes could be brought alive, than on the initial choice of the archetype.

... the challenge is to find an archetype that embodies the brand vision.

FINDING THE RIGHT BRAND VISION ARCHETYPE FOR THE MATURE BRAND

A mature brand typically suffers from a lack of emotional engagement. The consumers may find the brand boring, irrelevant or old-fashioned. Typically, there is nothing wrong with the products offered under the brand. Rather, the brand has matured.

The most important challenge is therefore to reconnect with the consumer by building an emotional connection.

The second challenge is to infuse energy into the brand. We have to change the way the consumer sees the brand as well as consumer behaviour (to get the consumer to buy our brand more often). As we want the consumer to change, we have to bring some energy to the party. A low-key approach won't work.

Mature brands typically do not represent any particular brand archetypes, but rather have fuzzy, fragmented brand images. Alternatively, they represent low-energy brand archetypes, such as:

- *Guardian*—organised, controlled, predictable, but lacking emotion

- *Patriarch*—setting the rules and standards, but drifting slowly into Shadow Archetype territory (the Dictator)

- *Companion*—always around, but not really engaging the consumer

- *Everyman/Everywoman*—for everyone and thus not special in any way

- *Soldier*—loyal and getting the job done, but lacking emotional engagement.

Contrast this with some high-energy brand archetypes:

- *Explorer*—exploring limits, pushing the envelope, learning more about capabilities and limits by giving it a go

- *Adventurer*—seeking thrills, trying the unknown, searching for excitement

- *Warrior*—fighting and winning the battle, unbeatable

- *Champion*—standing for a cause, relentlessly promoting the cause

- *Creator*—inventing better ways of doing things, breaking new ground.

I mentioned in an earlier section that one of the problems with a mature brand is that the consumer has stopped listening. The consumer has become indifferent, and turning indifference into engagement is the most difficult challenge a marketer can face. Significant energy is required to re-engage the consumer.

However, while energy is a prerequisite to effecting change, it may not be sufficient.

Unfortunately, sometimes a brand needs to stand for something that, in itself, is not of a high-energy nature. Because energy is needed to engage the consumer, we may need to introduce a secondary archetype to provide the energy the brand needs.

In other words, the high-energy brand archetype may end up as a secondary archetype, allowing the brand to break through the indifference barrier, while a low-energy brand vision archetype that expresses the dominant qualities of the brand takes the position of primary brand vision archetype.

The dominant qualities of the brand need to be of an emotional nature as the brand needs to reconnect emotionally with the consumer. Even if the product is utilitarian in nature, we need an emotional connection. Consider the Michelin advertisement showing a baby shower with friends giving the mother new Michelin tyres: 'because so much is riding on your tyres'. Clearly, the tyre is a 'guardian' from the utilitarian point of view, but the way the brand has been brought alive represents a 'friend' or 'lover' brand vision archetype.

In summary, when attempting to revitalise a mature brand it is important to consider the role of emotion as a central element. More specifically, we need emotional:

- *energy*—a force that allows us to break through the wall of indifference, making the consumer sit up and take note of what our brand has to offer

- *relevance*—the type of emotion that is in tune with the emotional benefit the consumer is seeking

- *depth*—emotion deep enough to truly touch the consumer.

The energy breaks down the barrier of indifference and connects; relevance engages; and emotional depth moves the consumer towards action.

Brand vision archetypes are a great way to develop an intuitive approach to repositioning the brand. Repositioning this way involves three steps:

1. An initial assessment of how the brand is positioned now in consumers' minds will allow us to establish if the brand already represents a brand archetype, or if the brand image is fuzzy and fragmented.

2. The next step is to establish a primary and a secondary brand vision archetype that will bring relevance to the brand and connect emotionally with the consumer.

3. The third step is to bring alive these brand vision
    archetypes at all key touchpoints in a high-energy
    way to break through the consumer's wall of
    indifference.

An important feature of brand vision archetypes is that they
represent a holistic, intuitive approach to understanding
your brand. This is something that cannot be achieved by
using a purely analytical approach, such
as brand pyramids or brand wheels.
Rather than spending untold hours
discussing which attributes would
best describe a brand, we can focus on
bringing a brand archetype alive that,
unlike a set of brand attributes, can be
intuitively understood by everyone: from the marketing
and sales team to corporate decision makers, from agencies
that have to contribute to bringing the brand alive, to
intermediaries such as retailers, and from influencers and
gatekeepers to the consumers purchasing and/or consuming
what we offer.

... brand vision archetypes ... represent a holistic, intuitive approach to understanding your brand.

KEY POINTS

- We think in images and 95 per cent of our thinking
  takes place unconsciously, yet we attempt to describe
  brands in a purely analytical, rational way.

- An analytical approach focuses our attention on
  details, while failing to deliver the big picture that
  would allow us to intuitively understand the brand.

- Jung and Campbell found that a limited number of mythic forms and characters can be found in just about all cultures from the earliest documentation of myth to today. These mythic forms and characters are called archetypes.

- We all 'know' the same archetypes and thus can communicate with others at a level that transcends language.

- Archetypes are not stereotypes. The latter are transient — they represent a type of person that may be typical in a particular context and time. Archetypes are permanently ingrained in our thinking, across time and cultures.

- Archetypes help us to understand where a brand is coming from, what it stands for today and what its future potential might be. The brand vision archetype expresses *who* we want our brand to be known as.

- Adopting a primary and a secondary archetype offers a number of advantages. The brand:

  - can address a wider range of requirements, aspirations and expectations

  - becomes somewhat less predictable and more interesting

  - can be strongly differentiated (primary archetype), yet still be seen to deliver the basic entry requirements (secondary archetype).

- It is important that one archetype is dominant while the other is only secondary. We want some tension between these archetypes, but we don't want ambiguity.

- The selection of a brand vision archetype cannot be delegated to the consumer. It is a challenge the custodians of the brand have to address.

- The use of brand archetypes is a valuable and highly effective way of developing a brand vision. It is in tune with the way we think—in images and patterns, rather than in words and analytical constructs.

CHAPTER 8

USE SYMBOLISM

S ymbolism allows us to increase the impact of the brand and express more effectively what the brand stands for by making the tangible intangible and vice versa.

MAKING THE TANGIBLE INTANGIBLE

Christensen[1] argues that product innovation cannot drive differentiation once the product's performance exceeds market requirements. This argument is compelling: why would consumers spend money on a product improvement if the product's performance already exceeds their requirements? However, sometimes a brand can express its (often functional) performance in an intangible way that

---

1   CM Christensen, *The Innovator's Dilemma*, Harvard Business School Press, 1997. CM Christensen & ME Raynor, *The Innovator's Solution*, Harvard Business School Press, 2003.

allows the consumer to indulge in the symbolic expression of that performance. Take cars, for example. There is little point in having ever-more powerful engines, faster acceleration and road-holding that approaches that of a Formula 1 racing car. Consumers in countries accounting for the vast share of car purchases simply cannot experience these benefits in congested urban environments, nor in the highly regulated and controlled traffic conditions of many developed countries (although there are still some German autobahns where you can let fly!).

Here, the aesthetic solution comes to the manufacturer's rescue: it is possible to express the power and agility of the car through design. In other words, the consumer can buy a visual expression of the benefits, even though the actual, tangible benefits cannot be experienced. As you walk towards your car you can *see* how powerful it is by taking in the aerodynamic design and powerful curves of its body. You may never experience your car at full speed, but its design allows you to nevertheless enjoy its performance.[2]

Clearly, we can sometimes escape commoditisation if design can express functional qualities that exceed market requirements. It is therefore no wonder that many product categories formerly comprised of brands positioned on the basis of superior performance are today led by brands positioned on the basis of design expressing this performance.

---

2   Note that we are using 'design' here in a broad sense, including the creation of any sensory input that creates the desired image in the consumer's mind. For example, the sound of the engine and exhaust can be a very important sensory input when it comes to sports cars. Similarly, designers can create an interior that is reminiscent of a racing car rather than a luxury vehicle, including the sensory experience when touching materials that are hard and masculine rather than soft and feminine.

Take home-entertainment systems. Let's face it: today's top-quality sound system can produce a quality of sound that most people's hearing cannot appreciate. However, design can clearly position a brand as unique and distinct, allowing the consumer to experience the quality of the equipment in a visual rather than auditory way, while making a statement about the consumer's appreciation of music.

Christensen suggests that a useful analysis of a product category is to identify those elements of the product where innovation has not yet exceeded market requirements. He quotes computers as an example: chip technology and software are the two elements where major progress that translates into meaningful and welcome consumer benefits can still be made. Forget the rest. No wonder that computer manufacturers make little margin, while chip and software providers (Intel and Microsoft) make so much money. This means that while faster chips and breakthrough software innovations are still welcomed by the marketplace, improvements in the hardware are not likely to be rewarded. This is why computer manufacturers are increasingly using design to express qualities that differentiate the product, from Acer's co-branding with Ferrari to a colourful range of Sony VAIO computers. The design can express the computer's capabilities or simply make visible the fact that the owner has chosen an advanced model.

... we can sometimes escape commoditisation if design can express functional qualities that exceed market requirements.

New design philosophies and directions change the appeal of existing design solutions. Importantly, by being exposed to different design approaches, consumers start to change their views on current (and past) designs. What may have looked like a snazzy design a few years ago now looks outdated. This is because designs are stored as memory patterns and new designs are evaluated against those stored patterns. A radically different design pattern may well lead to initial rejection due to the wide discrepancy between what the mind has stored as 'appealing' designs and the new design solution. However, once the mind gets used to the new design it is likely to make (some of) the old designs feel outdated. Thus, attitudes can shift over time from initial rejection to preference. The saying, 'it's grown on me', is a metaphor that reflects this process rather well.[3]

... attitudes can shift over time from initial rejection to preference.

Take BMW's new design style, which reviewers heavily criticised when it launched. Over time, it has changed the perceptions of many consumers. Today, an earlier BMW model looks quite outdated to consumers who have been conditioned by the new design style. The same applies to other brands that are still sticking with last generation's design styles. BMW's design has been a brave move, but, as should be clear by now, the revitalisation of mature brands is not a challenge for the faint-hearted.

In summary, new designs that consumers have been exposed to are likely to change the aesthetic impact of existing designs. And, importantly, design can be a means

---

3   The fact that consumers judge new products, services, designs, ideas or concepts against what they have experienced in the past explains why great breakthrough ideas rarely do well in consumer research.

of making the tangible intangible and thus making key product benefits meaningful and relevant.

MAKING THE INTANGIBLE TANGIBLE

Cars, mobile phones, computers, tyres and many other products offer tangible benefits. However, for reasons outlined earlier, they may need to express these in intangible ways because the consumer can't actually experience these benefits. But it is not always a matter of making the tangible intangible to symbolically present it. Sometimes, brands need to work the other way round, that is, to make the intangible tangible. This is obviously the case with offers that are intangible to start with, such as services, or where a tangible product benefit can be neither seen nor experienced in any other sensory way. One can see plenty of examples on supermarket shelves. For example, how do you market healthier variations of processed food items? In all likelihood you can't use any of your senses — sight, sound, taste, smell or touch — to experience a 'healthier' processed food item. Barring a psychological effect, you are also not likely to feel healthier as soon as you have consumed it. So how can a brand express such an intangible benefit? Graphics used on our packaging may allow us in this instance to symbolically represent this benefit — a benefit that exists, but cannot be experienced.

Other brands attempt to take a position that is based on values or other intangible factors. Take Dove's campaign highlighting that real beauty is natural. It is all very well to claim that Dove stands for real beauty. But today's consumers are not as gullible as the consumer was some

30 or 40 years ago. Today's consumer expects a brand to deliver tangible proof when making claims based on intangibles. Dove has established a Foundation that provides tangible evidence of the brand addressing problems resulting from the cosmetic industry's distorted concept of beauty. Importantly, there are tangible engagement opportunities on the Dove Foundation's website, allowing the consumer to not just listen to the brand expressing its values, but to participate in initiatives. This approach allows Dove to make its intangible value-based claim tangible.

Think about Red Bull. You may well experience an energy surge when consuming the product, but the claim made by the product is also made tangible through massive global sponsorships and the invention of extreme sports events that represent pure adrenaline, such as the Red Bull Air Race. These events help make the intangible energy claim tangible.

Attempts to make intangibles tangible also occur in the design of spaces.[4] For example, retail design often attempts to express an intangible brand positioning through a physical, tangible environment. The same applies to lobbies. From hotels to office buildings, architects often use the lobby to express the intangible positioning, whether it is prestige, modern, hip, functional or busy.

Proof that intangible experiences can be made tangible can even be found when taking delivery of a new car. Volkswagen Autostadt's famous car towers symbolise the excitement of taking delivery of a new Volkswagen.

4   See, for example, C Mikunda, *Brand Lands, Hot Spots & Cool Spaces: welcome to the third place and the total marketing experience*, Kogan Page, 2004.

Your car is stored in a car tower and is retrieved by a robot-like automated system when you personally attend to take delivery. The car tower makes tangible the excitement associated with taking delivery of your new car.

In China, where more than half of new car buyers are first-time car buyers, delivery ceremonies may take up the best part of a day. Again, these ceremonies make tangible the excitement inherent in taking possession of your new car.

I am reminded of a story I heard at some arts conference some years back. An artist was able to sell his paintings consistently above what might have been a reasonable market price. His secret was that he offered buyers of his paintings an impressive wooden box that contained white gloves. He told potential buyers that they should re-hang the paintings every year or so as light might damage them and that the white gloves were provided to make sure they did not damage their investment. This was simply a great way of making the value of the painting tangible by providing white gloves and creating a ritual.

Summary

There are numerous examples for making the intangible tangible and vice versa. In fact, more often than not, the question is: what is the right balance between intangible and tangible? There are clearly synergies. A claim based on an intangible benefit will typically become even more powerful when it is made tangible. A tangible benefit that cannot be experienced (or at least not at the time of making the purchase decision or when consuming the product) will typically be enhanced by the use of intangible symbolism.

In many ways this is simply a way of looking at a brand experience holistically. Design and brand activation should not be treated as functional areas that may add value, but rather as an integral part of the overall revitalisation approach that focuses on creating a holistic brand experience.

Of course, this applies not only to consumer markets; the same principles work in business-to-business markets. After all, the decision makers are still human and thus respond to the same stimuli and exposures. Leading consulting firms such as McKinsey make their expertise tangible by publishing the McKinsey Journal; Booz Allen Hamilton publishes its *strategy + business* journal as well as a book series under the same title; and right now, you are holding a book in the Mindshare *Strategy. Applied* series. And consulting firms that don't go that far are still likely to have glossy publications and presentations that attempt to make tangible their intangible expertise (at least until engaged).

> [Symbolism] allows brands to clarify their positioning and express their personality.

Given the importance of symbolism it is no surprise that design—from graphic to industrial—is experiencing a renaissance. Symbolism adds another layer of experiences and thus makes our world richer. At the same time, it allows brands to clarify their positioning and express their personality. As discussed in an earlier section, consumers are not likely to develop brand loyalty unless they really understand *who* the brand is. For many brands, design is an effective way of bringing the brand vision archetype alive, allowing the consumer to understand the brand in an intuitive, holistic way. Importantly, design can enrich the brand experience by complementing tangible with intangible elements.

KEY POINTS

- Product innovation becomes less effective as a differentiating factor when category performance exceeds the market's requirements. This point has been reached (in fact, long surpassed) by many industry sectors.

- An approach that should be considered is to make the tangible product offer intangible. For example, it is near impossible for the buyer of a powerful car to experience driving at top speed. But it is possible to express speed and power through design, thus allowing the consumer to savour the benefit through a different sensory input.

- Sometimes the solution lies in making the intangible tangible. This is important when the offer cannot be experienced, or at least not until after purchase. Examples range from package design to the design of retail spaces and the publication of books and journals by consulting firms.

- By combining tangible and intangible elements we can create a much more meaningful brand experience that may contribute significantly to the revitalisation of the brand.

CHAPTER 9

MOVE FROM EXPOSURE TO ENGAGEMENT

In the past we had to spend huge sums of money on research to find out more about consumers' interests, opinions, attitudes, preferences and behaviour, and the key factors that shape these. Typically, the research took place in an artificial environment that ensured that consumers did not think or behave as they normally would. In group discussions and interviews we asked them to explain behaviour they had never thought about—and certainly did not know the reasons for. And we created marketing metrics that favoured recall, as if recall had much to do with the impact of what consumers had been exposed to.

It was all a great mess really, and one should not be surprised at the multitude of studies suggesting that more than 80 per cent of new products fail, despite having been researched. In fact, it may well be that many of them failed *because* they had been researched, and consumers in artificial research settings had assured a moderator or interviewer that they would buy the product once launched. Not surprisingly, they didn't.

Finally, the world has changed. Today, we can simply listen in. More importantly, we can also participate in the discussion or provide a catalyst for engagement, such as a game, a website providing useful information, a competition that is fun to participate in, and so forth.

WHAT'S NEW?

Let's assume I want to get the main grocery buyers of households to buy from my chain of grocery stores. What could I do?

First, I can make ordering easy—with order forms, perhaps with frequently ordered items already listed up top. I can offer home delivery if desired or a drive-through/ pick-up option at the grocery store. Second, I can add value to the core transaction. Maybe a competition that ties in with some key brands (which will pay for the cost of the competition). I can design the competition like a game; perhaps something like a treasure hunt where slogans have to be matched to the brands that use them, thus ensuring the main grocery buyer spends more time with my offer. Recipes will almost certainly be a winner. And something like a 'Seven Roads to Health' pamphlet will surely add value too!

What else does a main grocery buyer want to know about? What about a section on first aid, emphasising the sorts of injuries that tend to happen in a home or garden setting? Horoscopes are always a winner, so let's add them! Cleaning guidelines may be seen as useful, in particular some obscure approaches to cleaning the most difficult stains. General household hints might include everything from dipping a banana in lemon before using it in a salad, to how to make aluminium shiny. Then maybe some note pages or places to record significant dates like birthdays and anniversaries. And, to round it off, a diary with public holidays.

This would make a nice website. But what I have described is a printed booklet published by the Independent Grocery Association *more than 50 years ago*. It has all been done before. The booklet in question was named *Martha* and the cover promised that *Martha* would save time, money and inconvenience—in that order. Doesn't it sound familiar?

You would be right to argue that I have taken an example that would fit Web 1.0, a web that was essentially 'read only'. Now with Web 2.0 we have an opportunity for real interaction and we can do what *Martha* couldn't—we can engage with the consumer rather than just expose her;

Without doubt, we can do a lot more to engage consumers today with the new media options available to us.

give her something to interact with, or simply listen in and learn. Yet many marketers are simply doing 'Martha online', rather than developing initiatives that would truly engage.

At the same time, we should acknowledge that nothing is really new. Without doubt, we can do a lot more to engage consumers today with the new media options available to us. But when we do that, we are tapping into very basic human needs and wants just as we have done for centuries. Our challenge is not to change the fundamentals of marketing, but rather to adapt our strategies and executions, allowing us to use new digital media options that facilitate engagement in a more effective and efficient way than traditional media could. It is a matter of extending our horizons and our work practices. Everyone can do it and it's not even difficult. In fact, with our marketing toolkit expanding we are now facing an easier task than ever before.

No doubt we can do more today. But reports suggest that marketing practice is only changing very slowly. In fact, Booz Allen Hamilton reports that the top 100 advertisers in the United States allocated only 5 per cent of their total spending to digital media in 2006.[1] What is holding us back?

THE NEED TO CHANGE WORK PRACTICES

Traditionally, advertising was based on an exposure model. An advertising agency would pre-prepare the exposure (here we will simply refer to it as an ad) and, once fully produced, it would be placed with the most appropriate media to reach the intended audience.

Work practices were developed to suit this approach. Over time, these evolved into lengthy, process-driven systems that took on a life of their own. Planning cycles are typically long and designed to be staged on a yearly basis. Campaigns are planned many months ahead of their

---

1   C Vollmer with G Precourt, *Always On: advertising, marketing, and media in an era of consumer control*, strategy + business series, McGraw Hill, 2008, p. 8.

implementation. And, while the parties participating in this process typically complain about time pressure and lack of time, the truth is that they have plenty of it.

The engagement model works quite differently. In this model, a brand's communications provide a catalyst that allows the consumer to engage. And when we say engage we don't mean just click on a banner ad, which is simply interacting rather than truly engaging. Engagement happens when consumers actually immerse themselves in the task, such as posting their own ideas on a site, conversing with other consumers in a forum, or completing a survey.

The idea is that, once the consumer engages, we respond to this engagement. We are in fact interacting with the consumer—or at least we should be. This means that much of our campaign can't be planned, designed and executed ahead of time. We have to be quick on our feet. To exploit the full potential benefits of our engagement with the consumer we need to respond to what the consumer is doing, and respond immediately.

To enable us to do this, we not only have real-time access to what the consumer says, we also have real-time metrics that allow us to monitor consumers as they engage with us. These metrics help us to identify patterns and, as soon as these patterns emerge, we should respond. If we simply put the metrics data aside as input for the next planning cycle—as we typically did under the old model—we fail to take advantage of digital engagement opportunities.

Having said all this I probably should clarify: there are some digital options that simply allow us to do what we have done before. We may be more cost-efficient because we can improve targeting, but we are still only transporting the old way of doing things into a digital environment. Take banner ads, for example. Essentially, they represent an exposure. There may be a small interaction opportunity via the need to click on the banner ad to get more information. That's vastly more time efficient and convenient from the consumer's point of view than, say, a magazine ad with a phone number or web address. But the principle is still the same.

The success of banner ads is not due to their ability to engage the consumer, but their ability to *target* the consumer more accurately and at lower cost. Ad serving is the new science that allows us to expose consumers who are highly likely to be interested in the type of offer we have. Targeting more accurately improves the overall effectiveness of our spending. It also lifts the percentage of consumers taking action or at least taking note of our communications, simply by making sure that the right consumers are exposed to our banner ad. But if we want to communicate with a specific, individual consumer who is in the market for our offer, the banner ad is no more likely to engage this consumer than a conventional print ad. It is largely the improved targeting that makes the difference, as we can typically be far more effective in reaching the consumer we want to talk to than we can with print advertising.

It's also worth noting that pioneers tend to get the best responses. Imagine how consumers would have reacted when banner ads appeared for the first time. Curiosity alone would have encouraged them to explore by clicking on the ad. But once they have been exposed to thousands of banner ads they are less likely to even take in what the ads offer. So, not surprisingly, click-through rates have decreased over time, but the relevance of the audience clicking through should in fact have improved as those who were curious about the banner ad, rather than the advertised brand or product, are no longer likely to give a banner ad their attention.

The ability to measure the effectiveness of online behaviour has contributed to the success of digital media, which is growing significantly, albeit from a small base. However, I believe the real-time measurement and the extensive set of metrics the digital environment delivers is largely a red herring that effectively throws many marketers off track.

What digital media allows for is measurement of behaviour in the digital environment. This is hardly the main issue unless the advertiser's core business is digital in nature. Measuring what consumers do on their website (time spent, on what, path taken through site, points of engagement, and so forth) is of critical value to MySpace, Facebook, Amazon and other companies whose core business is essentially digital. However, for the vast majority of corporations, digital is only a small component of the total media mix. The key challenge for these corporations' executives is to allocate their media spend *across* different media. To be able to measure behaviour in the digital sphere, even in real-time, is hardly a key benefit within this broader, strategic challenge.

... the real-time measurement and the extensive set of metrics the digital environment delivers is largely a red herring ...

The fact is that mixed exposures (where consumers are exposed to the message in more than one medium) are typically more effective than more exposures in the same medium. There is a mountain of case studies showing that managing the most effective combination of media is the key to success, not the finetuning of digital applications in isolation. Let us stress that the latter is useful and important—after all, who wants to accept wastage when it is possible to optimise?—but it is not the core strategic challenge for the vast majority of advertisers.

... to truly engage with the consumer in a digital environment requires the marketer to make fast decisions.

In this context I refer to Briggs and Stuart[2] who use a methodology that, first, doesn't focus on recall but on exposure and, second, allows the advertiser to optimise the media mix across all media. Their work seems to be worthwhile for building on, rather than getting carried away by, digital media metrics—unless the core business is digital in nature or digital accounts for the dominant share of the media used.

In any case, the main point I wish to make in this chapter is that to truly engage with the consumer in a digital environment requires the marketer to make fast decisions. There is little point in implementing a major engagement campaign while being unwilling or unable to make quick decisions, thus robbing the brand of its ability to respond to consumers who are engaging.

Unfortunately, however, marketers are notoriously unwilling to change their work practices. They like to fill out

2   R Briggs & G Stuart, *What Sticks: why most advertising fails and how to guarantee yours succeeds*, Kaplan Publishing, 2006.

brand pyramids and brand wheels, ponder the meaning of brand attributes, research everything that presents itself as a possible strategic direction, concept or idea, and generally mull over decisions for a long time. No wonder then that the typical marketer doesn't feel comfortable in an environment where engagement with consumers requires fast decisions. Existing work practices simply don't allow for that. *We believe it is work practices more than any other factor that is keeping marketers from exploiting the amazing opportunities offered by the digital world.*

Yet digital may present a great opportunity to revitalise the mature brand. This is true especially because it is in the early stages of development where we can surprise and delight more easily since much of the digital media potential has not yet been fully exploited.

THE IMPORTANCE OF STRATEGY

Wal-Mart sponsored 'Wal-Marting across America', a trip across America by Jim and Laura, a couple of adventurers, who stayed overnight in Wal-Mart car parks. Their travel blog reported meetings with wonderful Wal-Mart employees who were happy to work for this great American firm. Eventually it turned out that Laura's brother is a publicist whose firm represents Working Families for Wal-Mart.[3]

And let's not forget Subservient Chicken—a man in a chicken suit you can visit online that will follow just about any instruction you give it. The Subservient Chicken,

---

3   L Weber, *Marketing to the Social Web: how digital customer communities build your business*, Wiley, p. 6ff.

brainchild of the Miami advertising agency Crispin Porter
& Bogusky to promote Burger King, had 522 million hits
within 17 months and the agency won a Grand Clio in the
internet category for its work.[4]

But what are the underlying strategies for these
campaigns? What works, how well and why? These
are the big questions. While official figures are hard
to come by, there seems to be consensus among many
marketers that Subservient Chicken has done well in
attracting website visitors, but has failed to do anything
to lift Burger King sales. Wal-Mart's sponsorship clearly
got a negative rather than positive result and damaged the
corporate reputation of the retailer.

Undoubtedly, hundreds of other campaigns have been
more successful than these. With any new media option
there is a learning curve, but as more experiences become
available there are also some general guidelines we can
extract.

Many marketers and their agencies let ideas, rather than
strategy, drive digital media. They focus on their traditional
advertising campaign and then wonder if there are some
cool ways for their idea to be applied in the digital space. Or,
even more likely, agencies bring ideas with award potential
to clients who fall in love with them even if they don't fit
the agreed strategy.

Clearly, one needs a lot of luck to just happen to come up
with ideas that would actually support the brand strategy
without even trying. There are a number of very good
reasons for this rather unsatisfactory situation.

---

4   Weber, p. 39.

First, there is often a lack of leadership and synchronisation with respect to media and creative content. Media houses are in charge of media selection and purchasing. Creative agencies are responsible for the content the media will carry. But what happens when the media and the content merge into a single entity? You can't prepare the content of a blog, chat group or engagement on a social networking site in advance, hand it over to the media house and let them 'place' it. This is what happens with traditional media. It is how these agencies used to work together. But who is in charge when the content needs to be shaped over time in response to how the consumer engages with it?

With any new media option there is a learning curve...

Public relations agencies have put up their hand, because they have expertise in managing a dialogue, albeit more often with the media than directly with the consumer. Digital shops also typically claim expertise in this area. Media houses are increasingly starting to establish digital divisions to take on these challenges. Some creative agencies have also started to test their mettle in these new environments. But without clear responsibilities and authorities we will see the target missed more often than not.

Second, we note that many creative agencies have hired staff with digital competence, but these new hires tend to be ideas (creative) people rather than strategy people. They simply add some ideas—and sometimes some very good ones—but not necessarily ideas that are in tune with the brand or communications strategy.

At the same time we find that many media houses have hired digital specialists who, while they tend to know all about digital media and what could be done, often don't see it as their business to develop the big ideas that will bring the communications strategy alive.

The outcome is that digital is often underused or badly used. This is a pity, as it offers the marketer an unprecedented opportunity to truly engage the consumer—not like *Martha* did 50 years ago in a one-way engagement, but in a truly interactive, meaningful engagement that brings the brand alive and develops a relationship between the brand and the consumer.

KEY POINTS

- In the past, all we could aim for was to *expose* the consumer to our message and hope that this would influence purchase behaviour. Today, we can *engage* with the consumer. The game is changing, offering us a much broader set of opportunities to build a relationship with the consumer.

- However, the new world of communications presents its own challenges. Most importantly, we need to change our work practices.

- In the past we pre-prepared communications campaigns at our leisure, often over several months, and then placed them into the media that would most effectively expose our target groups.

- But when we engage with the consumer we can't pre-plan what we do. The whole point is that we interact and respond. Unless we respond quickly we won't have an effective dialogue with our consumer.

- Long planning cycles, the perceived need to pre-prepare and test everything that reaches the consumer, and even the evaluation of advertising effectiveness on the basis of recall are all work practices that slow down progress in moving from exposure to engagement.

- There's a long way to go, but consumer engagement is potentially a great way of revitalising mature brands.

CHAPTER 10

DON'T ENGAGE IN CHANNEL-NEUTRAL PLANNING

Another major barrier to making effective use of media options in general, not just digital media, is the widespread adoption of channel-neutral planning or 'media neutrality'.

An agency that understands the strategic challenge that needs to be addressed, and which media options are most effective in addressing this challenge, would never engage in media-neutral planning. Rather, it would develop a communications strategy based on the media combination that most effectively addresses the communications challenge and would guide the creative process accordingly.

Let's for a moment divert and visit Shell's scenario planning, which provides us with a perfect analogy.

Shell's scenario planning technique considers a number of alternative long-term scenarios, each describing a particular operating environment (for example, a positive scenario, a negative scenario and a neutral scenario). Shell knows that none of these scenarios will eventuate, but that's not the point. Having developed these scenarios, Shell can test alternative strategies against each of them. Shell will then adopt the strategy that is not a total disaster under any of the scenarios it is tested in. Not the best strategy for the positive scenario, nor the best strategy for the negative scenario. In fact, not the best strategy for any particular scenario, but the strategy that is least disastrous in all of the scenarios that were considered.

This is essentially what media-neutral planning does. Rather than develop a strategy that works best given a particular set of media options, the agency develops a strategy that is workable—but not the best—with *any* media combination or option that might be selected. This leads to a sub-optimal result, just like Shell's scenario planning. However, this is where the similarities between media-neutral planning and Shell's scenario planning end.

Shell uses scenario planning to prepare long-term strategies with planning horizons of 20 to 30 years. It clearly is impossible to predict the operating environment Shell may face towards the end of the planning period (and that's typically the time when Shell needs to realise a strong positive cash flow to pay for its long-term investment). It therefore makes sense to adopt a 'workable' strategy that is likely to allow Shell to succeed, rather than a more risky strategy that may work really well under a certain scenario, but lead to disaster if that scenario doesn't materialise. Further, because of the long planning horizon, Shell has an opportunity to adapt its strategy over time as some of the key factors that determine the operating environment become more predictable.

Contrast this with planning a brand's next communications or marketing campaign. If we are any good at what we do we should be absolutely clear about our communications objective and the associated strategy. Given the short planning horizon, all the media options are known. We also know which media options are superior given our particular objectives. In other words, we can select the media options that are most effective in generating the particular results we are seeking. This in turn allows us to develop a creative idea and execution that will capitalise on the media we need to use. So why do we engage in media-neutral planning?

Let's use a specific example. Let's assume the challenge is to revitalise a mature brand by creating engagement. Our mature brand is well known, so awareness is not an issue. The market also knows about the product offer and, in fact, most consumers have bought our brand at some stage during their life. The problem is that our brand has lost relevance. It is seen as tired and boring. It is no longer seen as a relevant part of life. We decide that our challenge is to re-engage the consumer and thus our focus will be on engagement rather than exposure. We can immediately identify the media options that would allow us to maximise engagement. We also can decide right away that the main function that traditional media will need to fulfil is to drive consumers to the digital media that allow us to engage consumers. In other words, the content for the traditional media will depend very much on the core engagement idea, which will be delivered in the digital environment.

We can limit our digital media choice to two or three core options. Once we have done that, why would we give our creative department a media-neutral brief and ask them to come up with media-neutral ideas? Would we not expect to get far more effective results by asking them to develop a big engagement idea that will be delivered in one of two or three digital engagement environments? The only reason for not being specific, that is, for adopting a media-neutral approach, is if we lack the competence that allows us to think this through.

Similarly, when our challenge is to expose rather than to engage, why would we not ask our creative department for ideas that are most effective in the mainstream media we plan to use to gain maximum exposure? Why do we need a media-neutral idea that works in media we are not going to use if we want to maximise the desired impact?

The answer would seem to be simply that promising media-neutral ideas is a way for advertising agencies that lack digital competence to still 'play the game'.

From an advertising agency's point of view the important point is this: an agency that develops media-neutral ideas can hope to remain the lead creative agency even if some of the executions are developed by a digital shop rather than the creative agency. But an agency that simply admits that it lacks digital competence and thus won't be able to develop a digital campaign, even when engagement is the key challenge, will most likely lose creative leadership, and possibly the account. So media neutrality is a great way for creative agencies lacking strategic and creative digital capabilities to stay in the game — at least until their clients wake up to the fact that they are getting sub-optimal solutions.

From a process point of view the issue is that most clients believe they first need to get a big idea from their creative agency before they sort out the media options to deliver this idea. This made sense when there were few media options, but not in today's media environment. Rather, the client should very clearly define the campaign objective and then allow the media agency to identify the most appropriate media to carry the message. This allows for a media-specific rather than media-neutral brief to be delivered to the creative agency. This in turn allows the creative agency to develop an idea that is tailor-made to the core media choices rather than a sub-optimal idea that works in just about any media.

Again, we are looking at how practices have not kept up with the changing environment. The media landscape has changed more dramatically than ever before yet the conventional process of starting with the creative idea followed by the development of a media strategy (or, at best, a parallel development of both) is still a common practice today.

KEY POINTS

- While outdated work practices are slowing us down, new barriers are being built. Agencies that advocate channel-neutral planning blunt the effectiveness of communications.

- Channel-neutral planning delivers, by necessity, a campaign that does not capitalise on the specific strengths of any particular media, as the objective is to create ideas that will 'sort of' work in any media we happen to select.

- A more effective approach is to select the media that needs to play a key role on the basis of the communications or campaign objectives and to then create a big idea that will work particularly well in these key media.

- A related issue is that while a big idea needs to deliver a thread that links all communications, it is imperative to deliver the message in a way that capitalises on each media's exposure or engagement strengths.

CHAPTER 11

CHANGE THE RULES OF COMPETITION

Over time, new technologies, popular culture trends, consumer expectations, industry innovation and other factors change the rules of competition. Can these rules be proactively changed by a single brand?

CHANGE IS ALL AROUND US

We tend to focus on a small set of benefits when making a purchase decision. These may be implicit rather than explicit, that is, consumers may not consciously think about the benefits they are seeking. Worse than that, when asked why they made a particular purchase or express a particular preference, they tend to rationalise their behaviour or thinking. Partly this is due to the fact that we tend to analyse when asked to explain a decision or judgement that has been made in an intuitive, holistic mode, and partly due to not being aware of our deep-seated motivations.

The important point is that the benefits sought tend to change over time. They are not fixed. Here are a few examples.

Job seekers

Job seekers used to focus on their pay package or long-term career opportunities, but increasingly young people want their dream job today, not at some stage in the future. Many companies are responding to this demand by offering value-adds such as coffee machines, relaxation areas, on-site massages, yoga classes and much more. (Only a few companies are attempting to make the actual job more satisfying.) The recession we are experiencing at the time of writing may well change the key benefits job seekers want yet again.

Public transport

Previously seen as a cheap alternative to a private car, today public transport is slowly moving from the 'poor person's option' to a desirable choice for those who seek environmental benefits. Of course, in many cities, there is still a long way to go.

Cars

Cars used to be categorised with respect to either a set of performance metrics (reliability or price), but increasingly safety features are playing a role in evaluating options. Environmental considerations are also starting to gain momentum, but for many it is more the price of petrol than concern for the environment that leads them to choose fuel-efficient cars.

Food

Food used to be a taste/price equation, but increasingly health considerations are coming into play—although few consumers are prepared to trade-off taste for healthier food options. They will choose the healthier option, but only if it also delivers on taste.

Advertising

Take the following example from the business to business (B2B) market. Advertising used to be judged on the basis of how many consumers in the target group are exposed to the ad, but increasingly, marketers are interested in how many consumers engage (get involved, click on something, post a message, play a game and so on).

WHY ARE THE DESIRED BENEFITS CHANGING?

There are several factors that account for changes in the benefits consumers are seeking. First, we note that Maslow's Hierarchy of Needs suggests that once a lower level need is satisfied, we move to higher level needs. From the marketing perspective this means that consumers start to seek different benefits once lower level benefits have been satisfied.

There are also broader trends at work—often referred to as meta-trends—that change what consumers are seeking. Elsewhere we refer to the fact that each generation is smarter than the previous one. This is a meta-trend that is changing the marketplace. A smarter consumer is likely to seek more complexity because they find simplicity rather boring.

Here a note of caution is in order: it is easy to see a trend as some meta-trend that the corporation has no influence over. The truth is that it is often business that paves the way for such a trend, or at least reinforces and accelerates a meta-trend.

Take, for example, the shift from large to small cars. Without doubt, rising petrol prices and, to a lesser extent, environmental concerns have had a significant impact on the consumer's decision. However, we would suggest that one of the key drivers was in fact product innovation by manufacturers. Over the last decade, the leading car manufacturers have addressed the main barriers to buying a smaller car. For many consumers such a car was seen as a safety risk. In fact, in the 1980s, some of the car accident research institutions proclaimed that the one overriding determinant in the outcome of an accident was the size of the car. For any consumer who was at all safety conscious, buying a small car meant taking a great risk. Today, many small cars have five-star safety ratings. Some car manufacturers have in fact promoted small cars as being as safe as large cars.

A smarter consumer is likely to seek more complexity because they find simplicity rather boring.

It also used to be the case that small cars didn't have any of the desirable features offered by larger, more expensive cars. Today, small cars from leading manufacturers tend to offer (with few exceptions) the very same functional features that previously were reserved for large cars — or at least took many years to trickle down to smaller cars.

Manufacturers have also invested in design. Whereas previously new design styles and solutions were typically introduced, if not reserved for, the more expensive larger cars, we now see small cars with distinct, leading-edge designs. In some instances, they are even part of the product range that leads a change in the manufacturer's design style.

Given the above, we should not wonder that there is a trend towards smaller cars. We would suggest that rising petrol prices, smaller families and environmental concerns have all accelerated the trend towards smaller cars, but in fact it was the removal by car companies of the key barriers to buying a small car that facilitated this trend. In other words, if small cars were generally still unsafe, didn't offer the features consumers' desire, and sported outdated or boring designs, we would not have experienced the massive move away from large towards smaller cars.

The interesting question is: what did the car industry think while they were improving their small car offers? Did they really believe this would have little impact on the consumer's decision on what to buy? The current trend towards small cars has been in the making for a long time, by the car industry itself.

It is a useful exercise for any company to consider how developments in their industry sector may be changing consumer choice over the long term. In particular, we need to ask whether these developments are likely to change either the benefits consumers are seeking, or the options open to the consumer when it comes to buying these benefits.

Can we proactively change criteria?

Once we agree that the benefits sought change over time, it is only a small step to raise the question: can we *proactively* change what consumers are seeking in a way that revitalises our brand?

There are indeed examples of brands that have been able to do just that.

From number of people to *relevant* number of people

Let's start with a compelling B2B example. Buchholz and Woerdeman[1] present RTL as a case in point when it comes to changing the benefits the market is seeking. RTL was the first private German television station. When founded, it faced massive competitors in the form of established public television stations. RTL did not have the audience numbers to compete effectively with these behemoths. Rather than seeing this as a battle it could not win and giving up, RTL decided to actively change the benefits media buyers sought.

At that time, media buyers were simply interested in the size of audiences. RTL started to promote what it called 'the advertising relevant target group' which it defined as aged from 14 to 49 years—a demographic segment RTL did well with. Over time, this became the benefit many

---

1   A Buchholz & W Wördemann, *Spielstrategies im Business: Die Regeln des Wettbewerbs verändern*, Campus, 2008.

advertisers started to seek when making media choices. While it often didn't really make sense, given that the 50-plus age group is a major buyer of a wide range of products and services and has unparalleled spending power, it nevertheless became a key focus that changed the decisions made by marketers and media buyers alike.

This strategy rendered some 70 per cent of ARD's (the market leader) audience irrelevant, as they did not fit into the 14- to 49-year-old segment and thus turned RTL, with its young audience profile, into a valued media option.[2]

This is an example where there was no meta-trend facilitating a change in benefits sought. Rather, it was the company that changed the rules of competition.

From watching a movie to a total entertainment experience

We can find another example in the cinema industry. Cinemas used to be selected on the basis of convenience given that the movies are the same everywhere, but today there is a growing segment of consumers seeking a total entertainment experience (for example, recliner seats, food and drink during the performance and so on). This has allowed cinemas to rejuvenate their offering and to charge a premium price for a total entertainment experience.

From performance to style

Laptops used to be selected on the basis of a set of performance criteria, but today weight and design have

---

2   Von Clausewitz would have been proud of RTL. The company did not accept the objective point but rather searched for the decisive point and, by doing so, changed the rules of the game.

become important benefits to an increasing number of buyers. This change in criteria has been triggered by new product launches and promotional campaigns.

From a brand that offers effective products to a brand that understands me

Of course Dove, a case example I referred to in an earlier chapter, would also fit into this section. Dove changed the benefit from 'Does this product work?' or 'Does this brand express the image I am aspiring to?' to 'Does this brand understand me?'

From functional to behavioural benefits

Another great example is the change in criteria from 'Does this nappy deliver the functional benefits I am seeking (dryness, no nappy rash, ease of application)?' to 'Does this nappy help me to toilet-train my toddler?' These are very different benefits and Huggies as well as Pampers have been able to convince consumers that the latter benefit is important.

Huggies launched toilet-training nappies for toddlers: Huggies Pull-Ups. These are designed like underpants for toddlers and have a special feature called the 'Feel Wet To Learn'—a wetness liner that ensures the toddler feels wet rather than the nappy immediately absorbing the liquid. On its website Huggies dedicates a section to toilet training,[3] covering aspects such as:

- facts about toilet training

- toddlers' point of view on toilet training

---

3   <http://huggies.com.au/beingaparent/toilettraining/default.asp>

- parents' forum for discussion
- how to know when to begin toilet training your child
- tips on toilet training your child
- motivating your child to use the toilet
- potential issues that may arise from toilet training
- toilet training guide redeemable with a Huggies Pull-Ups Training Pants barcode.

Pampers also has a section on its website devoted to potty training[4] and a product brand, Pampers Easy Ups Trainers with a 'Feel 'n Learn' liner that is designed to deliver this benefit. There is little doubt that these manufacturers are changing the benefits many parents are seeking when buying nappies for their toddler.

From entertainment to self-development

As a final example, let's consider game consoles that offered entertainment value as the key benefit, typically referred to as 'computer games', with Sony PlayStation and Microsoft's Xbox dominant in this category.

When Nintendo launched Wii it changed the concept into a seemingly ever-expanding range of 'games' that add value to the consumer's life and lifestyle. There are programs that turn a fitness routine into a game, help users to keep their brain active and to train particular brain functions, help older people or those with sensory impairments to train their sensory organs, support people's efforts to cook great meals, and so on.

---

4   <www.pampers.com/en_US/learning/page/tpc_dev_potty_home/
     stageId/104.do>

Suddenly, the consumer is asking, 'what does this game do for me besides just entertaining me?' Undoubtedly, there are many consumers left who simply want to play a conventional computer game designed to entertain, but there is a growing number of consumers who are spending some of their discretionary income seeking new benefits that were traditionally not associated with computer games. Importantly, Nintendo has been able to tap into a significant segment of non-gamers by offering new benefits.

Suddenly, the consumer is asking, 'what does this game do for me besides just entertaining me?'

Core to Nintendo's success is its wireless controller, the Wii Remote, which can be used as a hand-held pointing device, detecting movement in three dimensions. Another, arguably less compelling benefit at this point in time is WiiConnect24, which enables the GameCube to receive messages and updates via the internet while in standby mode. However, this actual connection between the Wii user and Nintendo will allow the company to engage the consumer with its brand in myriad ways in the future.

Nintendo has publicly attributed the success of the Wii to Kim and Mauborgne's 'blue ocean strategy' concept.[5] The blue ocean concept suggests that a company, product or brand needs to be differentiated across key factors that drive purchase decisions, with the differentiation strong enough to create a highly differentiated positioning.

In the past, the key game console brands competed in what Kim and Mauborgne call 'red ocean', that is, territory red with blood due to fierce competition between brands

---

5   W Chan Kim & R Mauborgne, *Blue Ocean Strategy: how to create uncontested market space and make the competition irrelevant*, Harvard Business School Press, 2005.

and products offering largely the same types of benefits. Wii's differentiation on the basis of benefits migrates it to blue ocean, where no other (significant) brand is yet competing. In other words, it creates a new market where consumers seek benefits that are not available in the established game console market. To change the rules of competition, Wii:

- places more emphasis on the fun factor than technical advancement

- is intuitive and thus easy to use

- is designed to appeal not to regular gamers (which would have placed Wii in red ocean territory by having to deliver more of what this particular target group wants from games) but more broadly to people of all ages and interests

- doesn't offer the latest high-tech graphics

- requires less advanced hardware

- has a significantly lower price

- lacks the wide range of additional, often peripheral features that its competitors were constantly adding, such as movie-playing.

KEY POINTS

- We know that the benefits consumers seek change over time. The question is: how can we proactively drive this change to revitalise our mature brand?

- Sometimes it is a matter of focusing the consumer on higher level benefits in Maslow's Hierarchy of Needs, for example, to change the focus from the unctional benefits of nappies to benefits associated with child development.

- In some markets we can attract a significant number of consumers who don't engage by focusing on a different benefit. For example, many consumers who don't see themselves as hardcore computer game players and did not buy a Sony PlayStation or Microsoft Xbox were attracted to Nintendo's Wii GameCube because it offers a wider variety of non-traditional engagement opportunities that appeal to non-gamers.

Part III

Selecting the Strategy That's Right for You

In part II you hopefully identified a handful of strategic options you could develop and implement to revitalise a mature brand under your care. At this point, your focus is moving to selecting the strategy that's 'right' for you. There will undoubtedly be a number of factors that will inform the priorities you set, from budget limitations to the likelihood of the organisation embracing particular strategies. However, in my experience executives often overlook external macro-drivers that change the operating environment irreversibly.

A revitalisation strategy that is not in tune with these macro-drivers is not likely to succeed. It may bring some initial gains, but these are unlikely to be sustainable. It follows that you need to consider these drivers of change when choosing which revitalisation strategy to implement from the options you have identified.

Two key macro-level drivers that are of particular importance are *industry evolution* and the *consumer evolution*. A brand strategy that is not aligned with these evolutionary paths is likely to be ineffective. At the same time, the opposite also holds true: by aligning your revitalisation strategy with your industry's evolutionary path and by being in tune with the consumer's evolution you may be able to boost your strategy's effectiveness.

I will therefore begin this final part of our revitalisation journey by looking at industry evolution and the evolution of the consumer. There is, however, one overriding issue we need to consider: will your brand revitalisation strategy be able to change the brand construct in the consumer's mind? This question is not just relevant with respect to the strategic options you are considering, but extends to their implementation. You may have identified an effective revitalisation strategy, but if your implementation is too low-key it is not likely to change how consumers feel about the brand. This issue is of particular importance because consumers are often quite indifferent towards mature brands, even those they still buy habitually. You have to break through this barrier of indifference and change the consumer's brand perceptions. Needless to say, this is a necessary prerequisite for the success of your revitalisation efforts.

Chapter 12

Is your brand revitalisation strategy aligned with the industry's evolutionary path?

An industry's evolutionary path is a key driver that will impact on the corporation as a whole, and will therefore affect the success of the revitalisation strategy. Thus, we need to consider any revitalisation strategies we might adopt in light of the evolutionary path our industry is on.

Sometimes, a revitalisation strategy can help align the brand strategy with the industry's evolutionary path, as our case example will show. Sometimes it can even capitalise on industry evolution. But, most importantly, we need to avoid a situation where the revitalisation strategy is in conflict with the industry's evolutionary path. If such conflict arises there is every chance that any initial success the revitalisation efforts may bring will be short-lived. Sooner or later (typically sooner) we will find that developments at the industry level render the misaligned revitalisation strategy ineffective.

As you read this chapter, try to identify the evolutionary path your own industry is on. Then consider the revitalisation options you have identified in light of this path. This may allow you to identify and eliminate strategic options that are in conflict with this path, ensuring you don't build the future of your brand on a shaky foundation. It may also allow you to adapt strategic options to ensure such conflict can be avoided and even to develop implementation guidelines that guarantee you capitalise on broader industry developments.

CASE EXAMPLE

It is the year 2006. The weight loss market is growing — hardly a wonder, given the obesity crisis many nations are facing. Jenny Craig and Weight Watchers are two successful mature brands in this category.

The Atkins/South Beach low-carb diets shook up the weight loss market over the last few years. They reached their peak in 2004 and then started to decline. Jenny Craig and Weight Watchers rebounded. Jenny Craig was particularly successful with its advertising campaign featuring 'fat actress' Kirsty Alley, launching in early 2005.[1]

During this time we also saw an increased use of internet-based programs as an alternative source

---

1   *Commercial Weight Loss Programs — US*, Mintel Report, November 2005.

of diet help. Mintel estimated that in the US there were over 600 online diet plans on offer by 2005. The report notes that:

> *Some plans are branded subscription plans, such as eDiets, while others are subsidiaries of health-based organizations and offer limited but no-cost help ... While none of these programs is as comprehensive and detailed as a brick-and-mortar weight loss program, they can otherwise engage consumers who might be uneasy approaching a counsellor face to face.*
>
> *In addition, the popularity of weblogs, or 'blogs', has crossed into the diet and weight loss market as well. Hundreds, possibly thousands, of individuals create websites via free (Blogspot) or low-cost (Typepad) blog hosters to create a weight loss blog.*[2]

A 2006 Credit Suisse Report estimates that Weight Watchers' online business accounts for as much as 30 per cent of the total value of the company.

Let's now step back and look at this industry sector and some of the key developments:

- *Product innovation:* a new type of diet—the low-carb diet spearheaded by the Atkins diet—took significant market share over a period of several years, but did not revolutionise the diet industry in a lasting way.

- *Promotions:* effective advertising campaigns have proven to be capable of giving mature brands

---

2 *Commercial Weight Loss Programs—US.*

a significant boost, but not to deliver sustained revitalisation.

- *Delivery innovation:* there are clear signs that disintermediation through online delivery will revolutionise the industry.

In this context one might rightly ask: how successful is a revitalisation strategy that just creates a short- to medium-term burst without addressing the fundamental issues of industry evolution? Atkins with a revolutionary diet innovation versus Jenny Craig with a successful advertising campaign versus Weight Watchers establishing a successful online product presence with margins similar to those realised in its face-to-face/bricks-and-mortar business. Which company's revitalisation strategy is most likely to succeed?[3]

What we are seeing here is the importance of not just identifying possible revitalisation strategies, but selecting the right one(s)—the strategy or the strategy mix that will lead to a sustainable, long-term revitalisation of the brand.

Clearly, I am not suggesting that Jenny Craig's success was unimportant, nor insubstantial from the shareholders' point of view. Nevertheless, it was Weight Watchers that had developed a revitalisation program that aligned the company's strategy with the evolutionary changes taking place in its industry sector.

---

3   The Atkins Diet was, of course, a challenger rather than a revitalisation strategy. Nevertheless, it allowed us to understand the significant short-term impact product innovation can have as well as the lack of sustainability associated with product innovation that creates or exploits a fad.

There is little doubt that, long term, a revitalisation strategy will be more effective when it aligns a company and its brand with the evolutionary path the industry sector is on. Or, put differently, if disintermediation is the key factor that is changing your industry sector, you are well advised to select and implement a revitalisation strategy that deals with this development. If you fail to do so, you will find that your revitalisation is short-lived.

Having made this somewhat obvious observation, I note that industry evolution is rarely considered when a group of marketers and their agencies hold a revitalisation workshop — even less so when they attempt to 'brainstorm' a revitalisation solution that will magically boost their brand.

This leads us to the key issue: if your revitalisation strategy is not aligned with the evolutionary path your industry is on, then it may well revitalise the brand and the business in the short to medium term, but it is unlikely to achieve a long-term reversal of fortunes. Coming back to the case study I used earlier, we would expect that the future success of mature brands such as Weight Watchers and Jenny Craig will depend very much on the development of strategies that deal with the disintermediation taking place in this industry sector, driven primarily (but not exclusively) by new online services. Anyone who needs convincing should visit the Tesco website and check the diet programs on offer. Not only is there significant variety, there are programs for consumers with specific health concerns, for males and females, for consumers with a preference for a particular type of weight loss program. There is even a team of counsellors who will provide guidance and encouragement over the phone or via the internet.

You may remember the Nintendo Wii case study I used in an earlier section. Wii already offers cooking instructions and demonstrations as well as fitness programs and we would expect that integrated weight loss programs are not far behind. In other words, we can see a wide range of non-traditional competitors taking advantage of a growing potential market and the low entry barriers due to the possibility of online delivery. Others are using existing infrastructure already paid for by the core business, such as pharmacies or gyms offering weight loss programs.

For this reason, I believe it is of critical importance for any CEO or marketing director to ask themselves if their overall strategy is aligned with the evolutionary path their industry is on. And if there is alignment today, but an expectation that the industry will soon enter the next phase of evolution that will change the rules of the game, then the revitalisation program should be used as a means of becoming an early pioneer by aligning the company with the evolving next phase of industry evolution.

In summary, to select the most effective revitalisation option, it is important for the custodian of a brand to understand which evolutionary path the industry sector follows and which phase of evolution has been reached. This may sound like a massive undertaking, but due to the efforts of Anita McGahan and her collaborators, it actually is not.[4]

---

4   AM McGahan, *How Industries Evolve*, Harvard Business School Press, 2004.

INDUSTRY EVOLUTION

The research that provides the foundation for McGahan's work on industry evolution was carried out at the Harvard Business School, Stanford University, and Boston University over a 10-year period. More than 700 industries were analysed, assessing the industry effects on the profitability of businesses and the associated investor returns. We are therefore not dealing with some theoretical concept, but rather the results of empirical research.

McGahan identified four evolutionary paths and suggested that every industry sector can be classified into only one of these. These are:

- progressive

- radical

- intermediating

- creative.

Understanding the evolutionary path your industry is on allows you to 'see the implications of structural change before your competitors see them, and so use your existing strengths to achieve an enduring competitive advantage', suggests McGahan.[5] The fundamental difference in how the four evolutionary developments impact on companies lies in the threat they pose to the industry's *core activities and assets.*

McGahan defines assets as 'items with durable value that are the property of the firms in the industry' (factories,

5   AM McGahan, p. 1.

warehouses, particular skills and so on), and activities are defined as actions taken by firms to create profits. The word 'core' identifies an asset or activity as central to the value created by the industry.

Now, stop reading, take a piece of paper and list your industry's core activities and assets. Keep in mind that you need to focus on the industry you are part of, rather than your company.

... you need to question if assets, activities or even both are under threat given the way your industry is developing.

Once you have taken this step, you need to question if assets, activities or even both are under threat given the way your industry is developing. In other words, is your industry changing over time in a direction that renders key assets or key activities less valuable?

When threats occur to both core assets and core activities, then your industry is confronted with *radical* change. The absence of both types of threats means that your industry is changing *progressively*. When only core assets or core activities are under threat, then change is *creative* or *intermediating*, respectively.[5]

Clearly, the obsolescence of core assets and/or core activities is likely to lead to the maturity and then decline of brands and, in fact, the companies that own them. However, if these threats are due to industry-wide changes, then a rejuvenation strategy that is based on traditional industry conventions will *not* deliver sustainable revitalisation.

---

5 AM McGahan, pp. 10–11.

The key point within the context of revitalising mature brands is this: when selecting your revitalisation strategy for implementation you need to consider which strategic options are aligned with the evolutionary path your industry is on.

I will not deal with *progressive* change in this section as this is very much a 'business as usual' scenario. Let's briefly review the other three evolutionary paths you need to consider before committing to a particular revitalisation strategy.

Radical change

Radical change threatens both core activities and assets and is thus the most dramatic of all evolutionary paths. The typewriter industry is an example of radical change. Clearly, a maturing typewriter brand such as Triumph could have been revitalised temporarily as the industry went through maturity and decline, but without a significant change in product and market focus it would have been an impossible task to develop a revitalisation strategy that would have been effective in the long term.

Digital developments have largely facilitated intermediate change (which I discuss in a later section), but occasionally we can see radical change occurring due to a competitor finding a disruptive digital solution. Wikipedia is such an example. Wikipedia changes not just the way a product is distributed, but revolutionises product development, pricing and distribution. This is a totally new business model rather than an attempt at disintermediating traditional encyclopedias. It is a case of radical change.

Creative change

Creative change threatens core assets but not core activities. Take, for example, the advertising industry. The core assets of traditional agencies are threatened by the trend to digital media which elevates expertise in this evolving communications channel above that of creating ads that work in traditional media. Needless to say, the skills and associated assets required (for example, a TV production department, print department, proprietary planning and research methodologies) are very different.

It has become quite clear that there is a slow, but consistent, move from traditional to digital media and, with it, a move from exposure to engagement. Agencies that have understood this evolutionary path have invested heavily in fully integrated digital capabilities and in developing their ability to engage with consumers over time, rather than just 'package up' communications designed to simply expose consumers.

Goodby Silverstein, for example, claims to have trained its entire staff to ensure they are competent when facing digital opportunities, an investment that has apparently paid off handsomely in terms of the agency's success. In other words, sometimes simply aligning your strategy with the industry's evolutionary path can revitalise your brand.

... sometimes simply aligning your strategy with the industry's evolutionary path can revitalise your brand.

It's also worth noting that in the digital environment the medium is just as important as the ad it carries and thus a number of agency networks have started to develop their media capabilities. While at this stage most of them simply employ some channel planners, there are others who have started to bring media back in-house.

There are, of course, many examples of creative change. Consider the emergence and growth of biotechnology versus the pharmaceutical industry. Both are facing the same challenges on the market-facing side of the operation, but R&D and production are totally different.

The speed of change is obviously an important consideration. We would expect the evolution of an industry such as advertising to progress quite quickly, given that there are no long-term fixed assets of any significance. The rise of biotechnology will be slow and it will not replace the traditional pharmaceutical industry, but gene technology may in fact overtake both over the next 20 to 30 years. We could look at the power industry and see a move to green energy that requires totally different skills, assets and competencies on the production side, but again, the change will be slow. In fact, substitution will be limited because of the overall growth in global energy demand. Yet, the evolutionary path is quite clear and a number of power generators have started to diversify their energy portfolio accordingly.

The key point in the context of our discussion is that revitalisation can be successful even when it is not aligned with the industry's evolutionary path, but it is most unlikely that this success will have longevity.

Intermediating change

Intermediating change threatens an industry's core activities and therefore jeopardises the firm's relationship with buyers and with long-term suppliers. Again, it is not difficult to identify many other examples, from online classifieds, online banking, travel services and so on.

A high profile example is iTunes, which essentially represents a disintermediation of the music industry by revolutionising the pricing and distribution of music. Or one might consider traditional media being disintermediated by digital media—both need content and advertisers but pricing and distribution are again where the difference lies.

In all these instances, the online competitors are not replacing the underlying business model with a new, all-encompassing model. Rather, they pick the part of the value chain where they can provide more value or the same value at lower cost (where cost is not just dollars, but could be time and energy—more about this in a later section).

The question that needs to be asked is whether developments of this nature represent a competitive move by one or more competitors that will lead to a realignment of market shares, or whether they herald an evolutionary change in the industry.

Let's briefly return to the Amazon example I used in an earlier section. No doubt Amazon has taken a section of the bookseller's value chain and transformed it into a more efficient and effective process.

Despite Amazon's undisputed success I don't believe that bricks-and-mortar bookstores will become redundant. Rather, I would suggest that this represents an aggressive, competitive move by a new competitor with a different business model, rather than a sign of intermediating change that will change the industry.

Obviously, it is important to understand if a particular development represents a competitive move or is a sign of industry change. Sometimes the answer is obvious; at other times we need to make a judgement. But one thing is for sure: your revitalisation strategy needs to be informed by industry evolution to result in long-term success.

CONCLUSIONS

When embarking on a major revitalisation project, one should not just look at where industry evolution is right now and to what extent the brand strategy is aligned with this evolutionary path. It may also pay to consider how industry evolution is likely to progress. The revitalisation program can be used to close a gap between the industry and the company, but it can also be a catalyst for propelling the brand into a leadership position by becoming a pioneer that represents the next phase of industry evolution.

... it is important to understand if a particular development represents a competitive move or is a sign of industry change.

With respect to the pioneering role, it is important, however, not to move too far ahead of where things are. There are numerous examples of early pioneer projects that died because the market was just not ready for the new concepts, products and services offered. Think of the early PDAs and the lack of market acceptance. The problem is not that there is no value in being first. The problem is

that if you get too far ahead of where the market is you will
be punished.

KEY POINTS

- A revitalisation strategy may have a short- to
  medium-term impact by simply generating some
  excitement or even by doing the unexpected.
  However, to have long-term impact it must be
  aligned with the industry's evolutionary path.

- Each industry fits into *only one* of four evolutionary
  paths: progressive, radical, intermediating and
  creative. It is important to work out which
  evolutionary path your industry is on to ensure
  your revitalisation strategy is in tune with industry
  evolution.

- Sometimes there is an opportunity to align the brand
  with the next phase of industry evolution, that is, for
  the brand to take on the role of pioneer. However,
  it is important not to get too far ahead of where
  the market is today, as consumers are invariably
  conservative in their choices.

CHAPTER 13

IS YOUR BRAND REVITALISATION STRATEGY ALIGNED WITH THE CONSUMER'S EVOLUTION?

Marketers are usually vigilant when it comes to monitoring consumers' attitudes, opinions, beliefs and preferences. However, their focus is typically on the short-term: how has the consumer changed since the last planning cycle or campaign? These efforts result in the identification of incremental changes, and a focus on these often limits the attention given to the bigger picture.

Over time, many incremental changes lead to significant changes in how consumers think, make decisions and act. As the brand revitalisation strategy is supposed to have longevity, we need to take these trends and developments into account when reviewing strategic options, and even more so when we embark on implementing the preferred option.

In this chapter I will focus on three tectonic changes that have gathered pace over the last decade or so: the consumer's ability to deal with complexity; changes in consumers' values that allow them to avoid conflicts between their personal situation and their values; and trade-off decisions that determine the purchases consumers make beyond those that are simply habitual.

CONSUMERS' ABILITY TO DEAL WITH COMPLEXITY

There is little doubt that the rate at which consumers are changing is accelerating. Most periods of change during the first three-quarters of last century were due to wars that brought major upheaval and economic hardship and uncertainty, followed by a period of reconstruction that offered entrepreneurial firms great opportunities.

However, the last quarter of last century and the beginning of this century were different. Change occurred mainly due to a higher standard of living that allowed many consumers to indulge and explore. This has not only led to problems such as obesity and a deteriorating work culture, it has also created a much more capable and powerful consumer.

It is a well-established fact that the brain will react to the intense and frequent use of certain capabilities by allocating more brain cells to extend these. For example, fMRI (functional Magnetic Resonance Imaging) studies have shown that London taxi drivers tend to have more neurons assigned to the spatial area in their brain than the average person, simply because they use this part of their brain regularly when imagining how they can get from one location to another.

The same principle applies to any activity, including those engaged in by the masses. Here are some indicators that highlight how consumers have increasingly been exposed to complexity and how they have learned to like dealing with complex challenges and problems.[1]

Electronic games

PacMan came with a game manual of 10 pages, while contemporary games such as EverQuest or Ultima have manuals with more than 200 pages and are supported by a wide range of publications that allow players to learn more about game strategies. Playing an advanced game is an activity that requires extensive learning, the processing of complex rules, and the evaluation of complex strategic options.

Movies and TV

There has been a steep increase in multithreading. While early TV shows delivered just one story in each episode, there are now many parallel and sometimes interlinking stories. Programs such as *ER*, *24* and *Lost* sometimes have 10 or more story threads in a single episode.

The same applies to movies that present biographical stories. For example, *Star Wars* had six biographical stories, from Han Solo to Ben Obi-Wan Kenobi. If this sounds like a fairly complex movie, try *Lord of the Rings*

---

1   The examples are largely drawn from S Johnson, *Everything Bad Is Good for You*, Penguin, 2006.

as a representative of the next generation blockbuster movie—it presents no less than 20 biographical stories.

There is also a decrease in what the industry calls 'flashing arrows', that is, explicit statements that explain to the audience what is happening. Today's audience is increasingly expected to work out for themselves what's going on and they would rather do that anyway.

Reality TV shows are introducing often complex and challenging situations. Viewers feel encouraged to consider what they might have done in these situations. In other words, reality shows often engage viewers by encouraging them to think through situations, rather than just passively watching what others do.

THE FLYNN EFFECT: WE ARE GETTING SMARTER

James Flynn, a New Zealand academic, provides tangible proof of consumers' growing ability to deal with complex challenges. He researched IQ test results up to 80 years back in some 14 countries. What he found was that every generation is smarter than the previous one.[2] In fact, IQs have been rising in developed countries by approximately 3 per cent per decade, and this growth is accelerating. More importantly, the questions in IQ tests on which later generations are doing better are those questions that assess fluid intelligence, that is, the ability to find practical solutions to problems.

---

2   JR Flynn, *What Is Intelligence? Beyond the Flynn Effect*, Cambridge University Press, 2007.

There has been quite a bit of speculation about the reasons for this trend. Overall, we can conclude that a person's IQ is profoundly shaped by the environment rather than genetics. And when it comes to the environment there is little doubt that each generation has experienced a much more diverse and challenging environment than the previous one. Just think about the toys children are given to play with. Today, even three-year-olds get electronic toys and it is quite common for five-year-olds to use the television set to watch DVDs or tap into pay-TV programs. In fact, when a parent can't work out a piece of equipment there is every chance a 10-year-old in the household can figure it out quite quickly.

The examples quoted earlier suggest that consumers easily get bored when facing conventional communication that doesn't challenge them. Obviously, a brand revitalisation strategy may not be based on a communications program, or its communications may rely on emotional rather than cognitive stimulation. But if it does rely on the latter, it must be sufficiently complex to allow the consumer to really get involved. Superficial communication is not likely to do the trick.

THE EVOLUTION OF CONSUMERS' VALUES

People's values change. This is important because mature brands are often built on the basis of values that once were widely held. Let's have a look at consumers' agreement with the statement, 'The most important thing about food is that it looks good, smells good and tastes good'.

Taking a 20-year time frame, you might have expected that, in light of the current obesity crisis, the number of consumers agreeing with this statement has declined. In fact, the opposite has happened.

According to NPD, a US-based research company, some 58 per cent of consumers agreed with this statement in 1985. The percentage agreeing dropped during the next couple of years, reaching a low of 52 per cent in 1987. Since then, there has been an upward trend and, by 2004, just over 70 per cent of consumers agreed.[3]

If your thinking was based on 'we have an obesity crisis, so surely consumers are now considering food from the weight or health point of view', you were wrong. If, on the other hand, you worked back from reality to the cause of this reality, you would have rightly concluded that 'we have an obesity crisis, which means an increasing number of consumers are most likely seeing the enjoyment of food as an important part of their lives'.

Let's have a look at one more question before leaving the obesity crisis. In the same surveys consumers were asked if they agreed with the statement, 'People who are not overweight look a lot more attractive'.

In 1985 some 55 per cent agreed, but by 2004 the proportion had dropped to 25 per cent. In a later section I will explore the fact that humans are natural pleasure seekers; here, the point I want to make is simply that we don't want to feel bad about ourselves. So, as we put on weight, we convince ourselves that being overweight doesn't necessarily make us look less attractive. By convincing

---

3   NPD PowerPoint presentation, 2004.

ourselves that this is the case we don't feel quite as bad as we shovel the next giant hamburger or cream bun into our mouths.

Here, we are not particularly concerned with short-term changes in values that simply express particular short-lived fashion trends. But when embarking on a revitalisation program we need to know if there is a long-term change in values that is in fact causing (or at least contributing to) the maturity of the brand. And we need to identify any emerging future values that might provide a platform for our rejuvenation program.

TRADE-OFF DECISIONS

The revitalisation strategy we implement must ultimately allow us to impact positively on consumer buying behaviour. It follows that an understanding of the key determinants of this behaviour is essential when it comes to judging the relative effectiveness of strategic options.

Habitual buying

In marketing we often assume that the consumer does make an active purchase decision and that this decision is largely determined by the relationship the consumer has with the brand. However, consumers tend to make many of their regular purchases on a routine basis. In other words, they don't make a purchase decision every time they buy, but rather habitually buy the same brand and product again and again. The original purchase decision that provided the foundation for the habitual buying behaviour may have been made many years ago.

This phenomenon has been studied extensively, especially in the FMCG category. I have already referred to Ehrenberg, the father of consumer panels, who has proven that repeat purchases are typically not a result of consumers' loyalty but of habits. True loyalty is based on consumers believing that the brand they buy is the best choice for them.[4] Habitual buying means that consumers don't think about whether the product or brand is the best choice for them but simply buy on the basis that it is satisfactory: they are happy enough with the offer and don't feel it is necessary to invest their time and energy into assessing alternatives and making a purchase decision.

... brands that rely largely on habitual buying need to be very careful ... when introducing the consumer to the joys of variety.

Most importantly, consumers do want to simplify their lives and the last thing they want is spend many hours, say, supermarket shopping, checking each choice to make sure it is the one that best meets their needs.

It is probably appropriate at this point to spend a few minutes exploring why flavour and size variations rarely lead to the revitalisation of brands that are bought habitually and, more often than not, accelerate decline.

The reason is simple: the consumer habitually buys the same brand and product without making a purchase decision. Suddenly, this brand offers a new flavour and, quite often, this flavour is promoted as something that is really worth trying. So the consumer who routinely

---

4   'Best' is obviously defined by the selection criteria consumers use and their perceptions regarding the brand's ability to deliver against these.

buys this brand may try the new flavour (or package/size variation).

When this happens the consumer first breaks habitual buying routines and, second, experiences the benefit of variety. As a consequence, they may well recognise the benefit of not always buying the same product without thinking. To have something a little different may in fact turn out to be quite pleasant. So what happens next is that the consumer starts to look for more change — some more variety or even excitement. And this means that the consumer starts to change from habitual purchasing to purchasing that is directed by an objective, in this case novelty.

At this point the consumer is likely to consider other brands as well. After all, they were never really brand loyal, they were just making a habitual purchase and so the change is not a major consideration. The above sequence explains why brands that rely largely on habitual buying need to be very careful when pushing the consumer into a purchase decision, and especially when introducing the consumer to the joys of variety.

Understanding trade-off decisions

Arguably the most important point from the perspective of brand revitalisation is that when consumers do make choices (that is, when they don't buy habitually), they tend to make trade-off decisions. This is of great importance. It means that unless we understand their trade-off decisions we will be struggling to influence these. To illustrate, consider the following responses from a Mintel survey on eating behaviour:

I try to eat healthier food these days	67%
I work at eating a well-balanced diet	58%
I consider my diet to be very healthy	44%

These results suggest that consumers are in fact quite health-conscious and making great progress with adopting healthy eating routines. Yet, in the same survey consumers also said:

I eat the foods I like regardless of calories	65%
There is nothing wrong with indulging in fattening foods	60%
I often feel I overeat	50%

What should we make of this? Are these consumers lying? Most likely, they are simply making trade-off decisions, an example of which might go something like this:

I like cake with cream. Yesterday, I felt like cake, but I thought maybe I should skip the cream. This means I have been trying to eat healthier food these days (no cream!) and I am working at eating a well-balanced diet (still a lot more work to do, but having no cream with my cake is certainly showing that I am working on it!). Maybe I don't quite consider my diet very healthy, but then again my answer will depend a lot on how ignorant I am when it comes to nutrition.

At the same time I can confirm that I eat the foods I like regardless of calories (I felt like cake and so I had a piece). And, quite frankly, while the cake is fattening there is nothing wrong with having it! Well, I probably had a piece that was a bit large (I thought I could do that as I was saving on the cream!) and so I felt I had overeaten a bit...

The point is that a consumer who makes trade-off decisions can truthfully respond positively to most, if not all, of the questions posed. Obviously, having answers to these questions doesn't tell us much about the specific trade-off decisions consumers make, and this is a deficiency with respect to traditional research methodologies that were designed for much less complex market environments.

Trade-off decisions lie at the very centre of purchase decision-making. It is essential that we investigate these, as only an understanding of these decisions provides us with an insight into how our brand is positioned in the marketplace and which factors we need to influence to revitalise our brand.

The Henley Centre, a high-level consulting firm based in London, suggests that consumers have five resources they draw on and spend in their day-to-day life: information, time, energy, money and space. The Henley Centre's approach opens the door to one of the most important trends in today's consumer society: *consumers are not spending less, nor do they have less to spend. But they are seeking better returns on the money, time, energy and information they spend.*

This invariably means that less has to be spent on some products, services or activities[5] which are deemed to offer low returns, to allow the consumer to spend more on those

---

5   We have included 'activities' as consumers sometimes get the benefits they are seeking from what they do rather than what they purchase. In other words, our brand may well compete with options that are free (although they will most likely require an investment of time and energy).

that are seen to offer potentially high returns because they add value to the consumer's life.

For example, today's consumer is quite happy to spend a few dollars on a coffee or fresh juice as a special treat, but will at the same time be attracted to a supermarket special saving her two dollars.[6] Many consumers are quite happy to wait for their drink for 10 or even 20 minutes at a juice bar, but will be outraged when forced to spend the same time in a checkout or bank branch queue.

The point is that consumers have started to use their resources more effectively. They have done this by deciding — explicitly or implicitly — to place some activities and purchases into their 'spend' and others into their 'save' category. The more savings made (in terms of money, time, energy, information) in the latter category, the more can be spent in the former.

In retailing this polarisation has been a reality for a long time: we talk about 'doing the shopping' when we refer to a shopping trip in the 'save' category and 'going shopping' when we refer to a pleasurable shopping trip we have placed in the 'spend' category because we enjoy it. Typically, 'doing the shopping' is based on a list (actual or mental) and the challenge is to tick off all the items while minimising the use of resources (money, time, energy). 'Going shopping', on the other hand, tends to be more exploratory in nature, is sometimes surprising, and typically enjoyable. 'Doing the shopping' is left brain,

---

6   The economic crisis that is unfolding at the time of writing has started to impact on trade-off decisions. Starbucks has lowered prices and closed underperforming stores. The economic uncertainty has led consumers to forego some of the trade-off benefits they allowed themselves to enjoy in a more secure past.

'going shopping' is right brain. One is rational and boring, the other emotional and engaging.

Clearly, the more a consumer can save on 'doing the shopping', the more she can spend on 'going shopping'. But the equation is much broader than that: the trade-off may lie in the purchase of an indulgence food or body-care item or time to sit down and enjoy a nice cup of coffee — all 'financed' by the savings in time, money and energy the consumer achieved when dealing with necessary tasks in the 'doing the shopping' category.

A strong price orientation when it comes to 'doing the shopping' is a natural by-product of the consumer's orientation. If a supermarket is seen to offer no sensory experience worth having, no fun, excitement, involvement, no feeling of success or deep satisfaction, then it will be placed into the 'save' category. From that moment on, the supermarket's sole role in the consumer's life is to save resources — money, time and energy — allowing the consumer to invest these resources in more rewarding activities.

WHAT IS A GREAT EXPERIENCE?

What defines a great experience depends very much on how a particular experience stacks up against an individual's past experiences. For example, black-and-white television had a significant impact when it was launched, but today it would have little if any appeal. Similarly, what young people used to find exciting a generation ago is very different from what they find exciting today, because today's youth have been — and continue to be — exposed to much more dynamic experiences which have changed their criteria for what is and isn't exciting.

The same principle applies to day-to-day exposures and the development of expectations. When you can withdraw money from an ATM within seconds, you find waiting in the bank branch more annoying than you ever did. In this way, new experiences and their particular sensory inputs can lead to a 'reclassification' of old memories and can also change the impact future sensory inputs will have. This is fundamental to any brand strategy.

But we need to broaden our horizons even further; so far we have only considered alternatives or competitors (for example, ATM versus branch banking, or Nintendo versus PlayStation). Clearly, products and brands are not considered in isolation. In fact, brands provide consumers with benefits which are judged relative to the benefits offered by:

- other brands in the same product category

- brands in different product categories

- activities that are not related to any brand, but that offer benefits that are similar to those offered by brands.

The reason is that all these brands and activities may offer very different experiences, but may nevertheless provide the same emotional core benefits, such as fun, excitement, being cared for, friendship, relaxation, indulgence, recognition and so on.

The question for the consumer is: where do I get the fun, excitement, caring, that I am seeking? And, *if the consumer*

*seeks fun and excitement, your brand competes with all other
affordable and available brands and activities that offer fun
and excitement, not just with brands that compete in the same
product category.*

Overall there is a trend towards experiences rather than
the purchase of goods. For example, a survey in Australia
showed that 35 per cent of adults said they would rather
spend their money on experiences than material goods and
85 per cent said that the way they spend their time is very
important to them as a source of pride.

These overall trends are very important, but we need
to become more specific if we want to develop a sound
platform for the development of a brand revitalisation
strategy.

The obvious tendency—at least for mentally healthy
consumers—will be to attempt to maximise their exposure
to brands and activities that deliver a highly intense, positive
experience of the type they are seeking. I referred to these
earlier as belonging to the 'spend' category.

There are, however, two restrictions consumers typically
face. First, there are necessary evils, activities that have to be
undertaken regardless of the benefits offered. Consumers
have to launder their clothes, buy groceries, develop some
skills, do (some) unrewarding work, carry out maintenance
jobs they dislike, and engage in dozens of other activities
they may not particularly enjoy. These are the 'have to do'
activities that are in the 'save' category I discussed earlier.

Second, consumers have limited resources. The money
and energy at their disposal and, most importantly, their
time are limited. One of the strategies they will employ

is to minimise their spending on anything in their 'save' category. This still leaves of course the question of how to invest the resources they have, to maximise the benefits they are seeking.

As a result, consumers trade-off between their 'save' and 'spend' categories. By spending less in the 'save' category they can spend more in the 'spend' category. Over time, they incrementally adjust their brand/activity portfolio to increase positive experiences. This means that they spend more time, energy and money with particular brands and activities that add value to their life and less of their limited resources with others that don't. The favoured brands will most likely span a wide range of different product categories.

If our brand has matured because consumers have increasingly placed it into the 'save' category then the challenge we are facing is how to deliver the benefits consumers are seeking. If we can't achieve this, we will fail to revitalise the brand.

But consumers also make trade-off decisions *within the 'spend' category*. Here, products, services and activities consumers believe will deliver the benefits sought are competing for the limited resources consumers have at their disposal, and any brand or activity that can deliver those benefits must be considered a competitor.

All of this is obvious. Yet, it is often overlooked when developing a marketing or communications strategy. And importantly, in the context of this book, it is often ignored when considering how to revitalise mature brands.

Addressing the challenge of winning the consumer's vote — first, to get into the 'spend' category and, second, to be chosen above other options in this category—is made even more difficult because of the dynamic changes taking place with respect to benefits sought as well as the increasing options of how to gain these benefits.

Essentially, consumers attempt to change their involvement with brands to their advantage. This is one of the fundamental reasons for brands reaching maturity. Once a brand is no longer the most effective way to get the positive, intense experience the consumer is looking for, it is doomed. It won't necessarily be deserted, but the consumer is likely to place the brand into the 'minimise use of time, money and energy' category. This decision will lead to maturity. It will also place the brand into the low-involvement, low-interest category, resulting in the consumer not being interested in hearing the brand's point of view.

> *… consumers attempt to change their involvement with brands to their advantage.*

On the positive side, this also means that we can revitalise a brand by adding emotional value to the brand experience. Most importantly, we need to reconnect the brand with what the consumer is seeking, that is, make it *relevant*.

KEY POINTS

- Consumers are becoming more and more adept at dealing with complexity, to the point where they now find simple contexts boring.

- Each generation is smarter than the previous one when it comes to solving practical problems. Thus, younger consumers are more likely to enjoy complex engagement and entertainment opportunities than older consumers.

- Consumers' values change over time. This partly reflects changing social, environmental and technological change, while values also change to allow the consumer to avoid facing up to personally threatening issues (for example, obesity).

- It is imperative that relevant values (values that have an impact on how a brand may be perceived) are understood and that the change in these values is tracked.

- Over time, consumers will adjust their purchasing behaviour, their involvement with brands and their engagement in various activities, in an effort to maximise the return they get.

- It therefore often makes sense to classify brands into the 'save' and 'spend' categories. The 'save' category includes the necessary evils, while the 'spend' category includes brands, products and activities that are enjoyable.

- It follows that the consumer will try to minimise resources spent on necessary evils and any activities and brands that offer only limited returns, while spending the freed-up resources on brands and activities that offer a more significant value-add.

- In the 'spend' category your brand is competing with all other brands, products and activities that are seen to offer the same benefits. These may stretch across a number of product categories.

- Revitalisation of a brand:

  ○ requires an understanding of where the brand stands with respect to consumers' current trade-offs

  ○ needs to impact positively on the factors that drive these trade-off decisions.

Chapter 14

Is your brand revitalisation strategy changing the brand construct in the consumer's mind?

Few would disagree with the notion that a brand exists in the mind of the consumer. It therefore makes sense to explore how a brand comes to be established in the consumer's mind and, over time, changes its qualities and what it stands for. Most importantly, we must explore how we need to change the construct in consumers' minds to revitalise a brand.

This means we need to examine how memories are formed (why and how we remember a brand) and how those memories are shaped over time (why and how brand perceptions change over time). To explore this theme more fully, we need to first establish a few ground rules—principles that govern how our minds work.

HOW THE MIND WORKS

When we consciously consider issues or consciously 'take something in', we are quite slow and limited. So how do we deal with the multitude of sensory inputs we experience every day? The simple answer is: we largely let our non-conscious mind deal with them. We are not consciously aware of the vast majority of sensory inputs our mind receives. Fortunately, our fast and powerful non-conscious mind sorts out these inputs.

Here is a simple exercise you can do:

> Close your eyes (without first trying to remember what you see). Then, with your eyes closed, try to remember the details of the room you are in or, if you are not alone in this room, try to recall the details of another person — their clothes and accessories (material, colours, style and so on), personal features (eye, hair and skin colour, facial features, body features).

> Now open your eyes and see what you have missed. Most likely you were not able to recall much detail.

Does this mean that your senses didn't transmit these details to your brain? You don't need to worry; your senses are automatically transmitting even the finest details. But your mind selected only a small range of sensory inputs to place into your memory.

In fact, your brain uses a chemical process that eliminates all sensory inputs that it deems to be of little relevance to you. You are not even aware of this process that takes place in your brain all the time. So it should not come as a surprise that some 95 per cent of our thinking occurs in the non-conscious mind. It happens, but we are not aware of what is happening.

This is fortunate, because our conscious mind is too slow and limited to deal with these sensory inputs. Imagine if you had to consciously consider every sensory input and decide whether to store it in memory or delete it. You would still be lying in your crib, trying to sort through the sensory inputs that accumulated during the first few months of your life, still making decisions on what to store and what to discard.

While you may consider it a great advantage to have a non-conscious mind that does this work for you, you may be less pleased about the limited capacity of your conscious mind when it comes to actively processing information.

Another simple exercise for you:

1. Say every third letter of the alphabet, backwards and forwards.

2. Start with the number 30, then multiply this number by three, divide it by two and keep doing just that (that is, multiply the number you get again by three, then divide by two, then multiply the new number again by three, divide by two, and so on). Write the resulting numbers down on a piece of paper.

3. With your spare hand, tap a melody.

You can complete each one of these tasks, no doubt. But now try to complete them concurrently, not one after the other. You will find that you can't do it. The human mind is actually not designed for multi-tasking. We can only consciously focus on one task at a time. To do more than one task means we have to switch from one task to the next and then back again, with time required in-between to adjust our focus.

There is an exception to this rule. We can 'automate' a task. This means we can become so familiar with the task that we can carry it out without giving it our conscious attention. For most people, driving a car is an automated task which frees them up to have a considered discussion while driving. Their brain will bring to their attention any unexpected occurrence that doesn't fit past driving patterns and they will then focus consciously on that matter. When this happens they will have to stop any other activity requiring conscious thinking, such as a conversation, until the issue has been resolved. In other words, the conscious attention switches temporarily from one task to another task and then back again, while it is our non-conscious mind that keeps monitoring and comparing events with past memory patterns, alerting us when something unusual occurs on the road.

... images are far more powerful than words: they reach our decision-making centre before the rational argument ...

Another important observation is that we think in images, not words. Our brain translates images into words and vice versa. This explains why images are far more powerful than words: they reach our decision-making centre before the rational argument reaches it.

But it is important to keep in mind that our brain doesn't just store images—the language of the mind—like a computer. Rather, it stores sensory inputs together with the emotions these sensory inputs generated as memory patterns.

In summary:

- our non-conscious mind is far more powerful than
  our conscious mind

- some 95 per cent of 'thinking' occurs in the
  non-conscious mind

- our non-conscious mind is largely responsible
  for determining what we store as a memory and
  what we discard

- we think in images, not in words

- memories are stored in patterns and include not only
  images, but also sensory inputs of all kinds and the
  emotions these inputs generated.

BRANDS ARE MEMORIES

You may well wonder where this discussion is leading. The
fact is that brands are memories. They are mental constructs,
based on past sensory inputs. In other words, *brands are
what we remember based on our past exposure to these brands,
plus other past experiences or exposures that provided the
context within which we experienced these brands.*

This is not a hypothesis, but a fact.

Why is the context so important? Imagine being introduced
to a brand by a trusted friend who makes a recommendation,
versus stumbling across a special offer promoting the brand.
Even if both the friend and the promotion stress the same
qualities of the brand, you would expect that the memory
might be quite different.

The consumer's mood also makes a difference to how a sensory input will be interpreted, whether it will be stored at all and, if stored, what qualities it will have associated with it. This is the reason why mood management has become a highly valued area of expertise. Retailers in particular often attempt to manage the consumer's mood through music, fragrance, colour, smiling staff and other means. The greeters that are often found at retail outlets (including financial institutions) in the United States are simply priming mechanisms: they are supposed to put consumers into a good mood as they enter the outlet.

But mood management is equally important when it comes to selecting television programs during which advertisements are to be screened. Consider a sad versus an exciting or funny television program; clearly, one would create a different mood in the audience and thus affect their receptiveness to various messages. It is therefore important to select, whenever possible, time slots where the audience's mood is likely to be in tune with your message.

But let us return to the core issues we need to understand:

- How are memories established in the consumer's mind?

- Why or how have consumers' memories changed in a way that led to the maturity of our brand?

- How do we need to change memories to revitalise our brand?

- How can we do this?

What is remembered?

We have already noted that not all exposures are stored, or
'remembered', by the brain. The brain has a way of cleaning
out sensory inputs that appear to be meaningless, via a
chemical reaction that eliminates the impact of a sensory
input. This is obviously a very important function of the
brain, as we cannot cope with all the input our senses
deliver. The obvious question to ask, then, is how we can
increase the likelihood of our message being:

- stored in memory

- linked closely to the brand

- activated frequently (thus strengthening the
  association between the message and the brand)?

Let us start by looking at the problem typically faced by
mature brands: they are low-interest brands. They usually
do not generate involvement. In fact, many products offered
by these brands are not given any attention as long as they
continue to 'work'. Consider household durables—as
long as your washing machine performs, you don't give
it any thought at all. Only when it fails is your attention
attracted.

Naturally, it is rather difficult to revitalise a brand that
stands for products of this nature, as the brand's chances
of having new touchpoints or exposures remembered are
slim. Yet, the storage of new impressions is obviously a
prerequisite for a change in brand perceptions. In other
words, revitalising a brand requires a change in the
consumer's memory, and such a change won't take place
unless we can get the consumer's mind to accept new

sensory inputs (exposures, touchpoint experiences) into the memory, thus changing the pre-existing brand memory.

Therefore, the critical question is, how can we improve the chances of a new exposure or touchpoint experience being remembered? All things being equal, we are more likely to store an exposure in memory that:

- *we become aware of.* If we are consciously aware of something and get involved, we are more likely to store the experience as a memory. This is why we speak of 'cut-through' in advertising. If the advertisement gains our attention and gets us consciously thinking about the product or brand, it is more likely to be linked to an existing memory pattern by being 'filed'—that is, etched on neurons as engrams—rather than the impressions being deleted because they are judged by our non-conscious mind to be irrelevant and of no interest.

- *is emotionally engaging.* Strong emotional involvement almost guarantees that the memory will be stored.

- *fits established memory patterns.* In this case, it is likely that the exposure will strengthen the existing pattern—not exactly what we want when the challenge is to revitalise the brand (that is, to change existing patterns). For example, if a mature brand is perceived as 'boring', the worst we can do is create exposures (such as ads) the consumer judges as boring. These will simply reinforce the way they see the brand.

- *contradicts an established memory pattern.* The mind is attracted to the unusual, to something that doesn't fit past experience. Thus, an exposure that contradicts an established memory pattern is more likely to generate attention and thus be stored. However, while contradictions may lead to a positive feeling of surprise, which would change established memory patterns in a positive way, they can also lead to a negative feeling of being deceived, resulting in rejection.

- *we have been primed for.* Priming creates expectations, which then provide a context when the brand is actually experienced. We will discuss priming in a later section.

- *is based on visual images rather than words.* Visual images are more likely to arouse emotions, are a fast-track to the brain's processing centre, and are more effective in communicating with the mind because the mind thinks in images, not words.

HOW WE REMEMBER

The human brain does not store information in serial form like a computer, but rather it builds a relational database from the very start. Different elements of an experience are stored in different parts of the brain and these memory units are connected. When one part of the experience is activated other elements are likely to be activated as well. The likelihood of activation depends on how strong the connections are.

For example, you may have had experiences similar to these:

- A particular smell reminds you of a holiday or of your childhood. As soon as this happens, images related to this particular situation or part of your life start surfacing in your mind and you remember fragments or even large parts of these experiences.

- You taste something that reminds you of another eating experience, leading to memories of where or with whom you had that meal.

- You may be waiting for service in a long queue and suddenly you recall other situations where you had to wait for a long time before being served.

You are *not* consciously trying to retrieve these flow-on memories. But when one memory unit is activated by a current experience or thought, your mind automatically activates other, connected memory units.

When you are exposed to a brand, you also store your memories in patterns. For example, if you were shown a bottle shaped like a traditional Coke bottle, you would most likely be reminded of Coke — your brain would retrieve this brand automatically because it is linked to the bottle shape. (Note the importance of differentiation: if you are shown a bottle of indistinct appearance, you are far less likely to retrieve memories of products or brands linked with this bottle — it is the differentiated bottle shape that triggers the retrieval of memories.) You may also recall — without being asked to and without trying — fragments of a Coke ad or a situation where you had a Coke. You may even find yourself in a good mood, because your mind retrieves the good-mood-feeling of a Coke ad, or the happy associations of a Coke-drinking occasion.

This happens because the brain, unlike a computer, not only stores information but also *feelings*; that is, sensations and emotional reactions. These feelings are very powerful and they are recalled just like other memories. This is why you may start to feel angry or tense when you think about a particularly bad experience. You don't just recall the information, but you recall and thus experience the feelings associated with that experience.

It follows that when you get upset while waiting in a queue at the checkout, you are not only likely to recall other occasions where you had to wait for a long time, but you are likely to also recall negative feelings, such as frustration and anger, which compound the negativity of your current situation.

THE ASYMMETRICAL WORLD WE LIVE IN

Merely delivering on consumers' expectations doesn't place the brand into a differentiated leadership position, it simply makes the brand acceptable (that is, places it into the 'herd elephant' position).

Consumers tend to give less attention to positive experiences than to negative ones. The reason is that we are primed to expect that a product will perform or that an experience will deliver certain benefits or qualities, so there's no reason to pay much attention unless something goes wrong. You don't look at your car tyres every day and praise them for their performance under the most trying conditions. As long as they work, you give them no further thought. Should they fail you, however, you will suddenly get quite strongly involved and blame the brand for its lack of performance.

We call this the asymmetrical world:

- when things work, we don't take it in
- when things don't work, we get emotionally involved and create a strong, negative memory.

An interesting point that needs to be given attention, particularly by the service industry, is the question of where the tipping point is. That is, at what point does a neutral experience change into a negative one?

Consider the queue at a checkout or retail bank counter. The consumer will give little attention to waiting time when it is short, but will get involved emotionally when the waiting time is perceived to be excessive. But at what point does the experience change from neutral and low involvement to negative and high involvement?

Bank of America did extensive research on this matter and found that customers waiting for up to three minutes underestimated their waiting time, while those waiting for more than three minutes grossly overestimated their waiting time and developed strong negative emotions. Importantly, the frustration generated by the waiting time will prime the consumer to interpret all sorts of experiences with the bank in a negative way. The bank will find itself on a downward spiral where the negative emotions will distort perceptions. Getting it all right will simply, over time, reduce and finally eliminate the negative associations, but they won't be replaced by positive associations. Getting everything right will, in most instances, simply mean that the bank will again be deemed to deliver an acceptable service—it will be a potential, but not a preferred, choice.

In this context we also need to look at priming again. If the consumer has been primed to expect fast service then it is likely that they will be more sensitive when delays occur. This is why it is bad practice to promote excellent service. This simply raises expectations. When delivering excellent service the consumer will simply accept your efforts as being in tune with what they expected. However, if you don't promote excellent service and deliver it, it will come as a surprise and thus make a positive impact. Of course, this can only happen if your service truly exceeds what the consumer would normally expect.

... we need to change the memory of the brand that is currently stored in consumers' minds.

REVITALISING MATURE BRANDS

Major mature brands already enjoy a high degree of awareness among consumers and few consumers would not have been exposed to them in one way or another, whether through signage, advertising, media reports, word-of-mouth, or a personal shopping or usage experience. For some reason, these brands have lost their sparkle—they have matured.

Our focus therefore needs to be on how the brand can be revitalised, which essentially means that *we need to change the memory of the brand that is currently stored in consumers' minds.*

We have already noted that memories are stored across various neurons. There are three simple rules that govern the changing of memories:

1. Connections grow stronger every time these neurons are activated together, that is, when the memory is evoked. For example, the memory of Coke and the Coke bottle shape are more closely tied together when consumers are more frequently exposed to both the Coke brand and the bottle.

2. Activation of one element can lead to the activation of the whole (or a larger part of) the memory. For example, whenever the consumer sees a Coke-shaped bottle, the Coke brand comes to mind, and vice versa.

3. When a memory is recalled it will be changed, either by simply changing the strength of the connections between neurons (and thus the strength of the associations between different elements of the memory) or by associating some new elements with the memory, thus changing the quality or meaning of that memory.

Here we find the essential challenge we face when attempting to revitalise a mature brand that is well established, but is seen to have lost relevance. Essentially, this means that consumers are now indifferent. They find the brand boring. They don't engage.

Simply droning on about the qualities of such a brand will simply activate the established memory pattern and strengthen the perception that the brand is boring and irrelevant. Our challenge is to change the existing memory pattern. But to do this, we first have to break through what I have earlier called a 'wall of indifference'. To break through this wall, we need to surprise and delight. We need to do something that exposes the consumer to our brand in a way that leads this consumer to think: 'Wow! I wouldn't have expected this from brand x!' To achieve this we either have to create a surprising engagement opportunity, a surprising touchpoint, a surprising product feature or a surprising message. When we say 'surprising' we don't mean in an absolute sense, but rather surprising for consumers in the context of how they currently see the brand.

Once we have broken through the consumer's wall of indifference we need to:

- *change the meaning of some elements of the existing memory.* For example, with a car brand we might change the focus from low fuel consumption to environmentally friendly

- *build new connections.* For example, link boring supermarket shopping to the excitement food can bring

- *weaken or eliminate existing memories or connections between memories.* This may be a strategy where we change the criteria consumers use when evaluating brands in our category.

Marketing communications are typically used to doing one or more of the above. For example, when we use advertising to build a brand's image, we are connecting the brand with positive memory units. These may be directly related to the brand (perhaps a particular product feature) or indirectly related (such as the social status we may gain by consuming or owning the brand). But memories are not only updated by mass media communications, but by every brand touchpoint.

In changing brand memories, we also have to make sure that the new inputs do not contradict the patterns that are already in the memory bank or, if there is a contradiction, that the new exposure is convincing enough to change the memory pattern.

The worst-case scenario is that a contradiction is taken into the conscious (which increases the likelihood that it is stored away, thus updating the memory pattern) *and not resolved*. A simple example: I believe (based on past exposures that are stored away as a memory pattern) that a particular department store provides poor service, and I have recently had a particularly bad service experience. I am exposed to an advertisement that depicts this department store as caring and putting its self-interest second to the customer's interest. I start to engage with this message, feel infuriated, and start swearing. The consequence: my brand memory pattern will be updated with an even more negative image component and the negative emotions will increase its power and impact when making decisions.

Herein lies a very important point when it comes to building a brand, especially when revitalising a brand that has lost credibility and is not trusted: *a positive message that directly contradicts the memory patterns for this brand is likely to be rejected and further damage the brand image.* This is, of course, not a new insight, but it may help us to develop a more effective approach once we take into account that brands are simply mental models, and how these mental models are developed and modified.

PRIMING

One of the most important opportunities open to us is priming. Priming essentially is a process that raises certain expectations in the consumer's mind and, by doing so, changes the way experiences are interpreted.

There are a number of common examples of priming that have been researched extensively. For example, taking a headache tablet is likely to have a positive impact on the headache well before the medication is actually active. The brain, being aware that a tablet is being taken and expecting that this tablet will have an impact, starts to reduce the pain level even before the medication could possibly have had any real impact.

Turning to an example more closely related to marketing: many used cars are sprayed with a fragrance that is similar to the characteristic smell of a brand new car. This smell primes potential buyers, who are likely to rate the used car far more favourably than they would have without the 'new car smell'.

There are also the classic 'taste tests' where a third-rate product is poured from a bottle showing a leading brand. Invariably, many consumers are primed by the label and expect a superior taste experience. They rate the taste much more favourably than their rating for the same product when it is served from a bottle showing the third-rate label.

To prime consumers we need to be confident about our offer, reinforce its benefits, present buyers or users as winners, show their enjoyment of the claimed benefits and, ideally, reinforce these messages at the point of decision making.

Another simple priming technique gaining attention in marketing circles is co-branding. This is simply a way of building a new connection between two memory constructs, that is, the two brands in question that will change the way our brand is perceived if, in fact, the connection is meaningful. At the same time the consumer will be primed by the new construct. For example, a Ferrari co-branded Acer notebook will prime the buyer to expect this notebook to be a top performer and to raise the eyebrows of others.

In summary then, how can we improve the chances of a new exposure or touchpoint experience being remembered and changing the existing brand construct in the consumer's mind in a positive and desirable way? We can say with certainty that any exposure that does not activate existing memory patterns will have absolutely no impact on the consumer's perceptions, attitudes, preferences or behaviour.[1] The vast majority of the brand exposures the

... any exposure that does not activate existing memory patterns will have absolutely no impact ...

---

1   Note that we refer to existing memory patterns rather than considering the development of new memory patterns as we can expect that major mature brands will already have manifested themselves in consumers' memories.

average consumer experiences are eliminated by a chemical process without reaching the brand memory pattern.

All things being equal, we are more likely to activate the brand memory pattern if:

- we become aware of the exposure (we are conscious of it)

- the exposure is emotionally engaging (taps into aspirations, fears, desires)

- the exposure does not simply reinforce existing memory patterns but adds a new, positive dimension to the current brand construct

- we have been primed for the exposure (for example, we have been told that this is a particularly positive experience)

- the exposure is based on visual images rather than words

- the exposure is dynamic rather than static

- the exposure is consistent with the mood at the time of the exposure (this is of special importance in the context of media planning).

When selecting from a range of strategic options that may allow you to revitalise your brand, make sure you consider the current brand construct in consumers' minds and what you might have to do to change this brand construct in a way that revitalises the brand.

In most instances you need exposures that have energy. You need to break through the boredom barrier. You need to surprise. At the same time you need to change the brand construct and/or link it with other constructs that give your brand desirable attributes in the consumer's mind.

It helps, of course, to first get an understanding of what the brand construct looks like. Here, I refer you to the work of Gerald Zaltman,[2] the father of consensus mapping, a research methodology that allows you to gain quite deep insights into the brand constructs consumers carry in their minds. You will be well prepared to judge the revitalisation options you have identified and select the option that will be most effective in changing the way the consumer thinks, when you have an intuitive understanding of the:

- 'map' in consumers' minds
- territory your brand owns (if any)
- territory it shares with other brands
- territory other brands (but not yours) own
- connections to other key constructs.

KEY POINTS

Brands mature for the following reasons:

- The memory of the brand is not evoked, or evoked too rarely (for example, through ineffective or a lack of marketing communications). This lack of activation of the brand construct will erode the connections between the various qualities the brand is associated with. In practical terms this means that the brand

---

2   G Zaltman, *How Customers Think*, Harvard Business School Press, 2003.

may still be remembered, but its qualities have faded. It has become a brand with an indistinct image.

- Brand exposures are so low-key, predictable and everyday that consumers don't become aware of the brand. The brand blends into the background and does not engage the consumer in any way.

- Exposures do not connect new, powerful and meaningful memories to the brand construct in consumers' minds. The brand becomes stale and loses emotional impact.

- The brand has failed to establish memory triggers or these triggers have lost impact (for example, the traditional Coke bottle is a memory trigger). This means that the brand memory is evoked less often.

- The attributes that used to differentiate the brand have become linked to other brands as well, and so are no longer 'owned' by the brand.

- The attributes or features that constitute the key benefit in the consumer's mind start to be more strongly associated with another brand. This is typically the case with fashion and fad brands.

- What the product offers has lost impact because competing offers provide far more intense experiences of the same kind. For example, using the latest generation Sony PlayStation may make the traditional Nintendo Game Boy feel slow and unexciting. Essentially this means that an even stronger link between Sony PlayStation and 'excitement' is established in the consumer's mind.

When excitement is activated, Sony PlayStation is activated, rather than Nintendo. This in turn leads to the link between PlayStation and excitement getting stronger, while the link between Nintendo and excitement weakens. The ultimate outcome is that the Nintendo brand will mature.

- The attributes that differentiate and/or define the brand have lost relevance. This may be due to competitors having changed the way consumers evaluate what brands offer through disruptive innovation. For example, Volvo was the pioneer in stressing safety as a key consideration when buying a car. This changed the way many consumers evaluated cars when making a purchase decision. Alternatively, the benefits offered by a brand can simply lose relevance due to changes in consumers' requirements or what they are looking for.

- A (small) number of touchpoints lead to (occasional) negative experiences that engage the consumer and dominate the brand memory. For example, long queues, long waiting times when ringing a customer service line, or unexpectedly poor product quality can dominate the way consumers feel about a brand.

JUST DO IT!

The most effective strategy is useless unless implemented. Yet, more often than not, resources are applied to the development of a strategy which, in the end, is not implemented as intended (or at all). I began this book by emphasising that there is no point in developing revitalisation strategies unless there is commitment to implementation, including the elimination of work practices that cause the maturity of brands. It seems fitting to return to the implementation issue at the end of our journey.

THE KNOWING-DOING GAP

Humans have an amazing ability to do nothing about addressing problems that potentially have dire future consequences. We are masters at adjusting our attitudes and behaviour to avoid having to act today when the payback is long term.

Take the way many people have adjusted to the obesity crisis by simply changing their attitudes towards obesity. As mentioned already, US consumers were asked in a survey if they agreed with the statement, 'People who are *not* overweight are a lot more attractive'. In 1985, 55 per cent of respondents agreed, while by 2004 only 25 per cent agreed. In a single generation, we have significantly changed our perceptions of how attractive fat is, effectively giving ourselves permission to be obese without feeling bad about it.

And then, if we can't convince ourselves that things are actually all right by changing our perspective, we typically take some inadequate action that will at least make us feel we've 'done the right thing'; such as going on yet another diet we don't really expect to work, because we've tried it unsuccessfully so many times before.

This situation is widely known as the 'knowing-doing gap', a phrase coined by Pfeffer and Sutton[1] who analysed the apparent inability of corporations to actually do what they knew needed to be done.

The 'knowing-doing gap' is part of the landscape of our lives. Take the education system. What are the most important skills the future generation will need? It is clearly not retaining a lot of information. More likely there will be a growing need for sense-making—for working out

---

1   J Pfeffer & RI Sutton, *The Knowing-Doing Gap*, Harvard Business School Press, 2000.

what all the vast pools of data, information and knowledge actually mean. And once we understand the meaning we will need to develop strategies for dealing with the issues and challenges we have identified. So sense-making and way-finding are going to be the key skills required in the future. Given this, why does the education system still put so much emphasis on retaining knowledge, while at the same time implementing strategies that appear to close the knowing-doing gap without really doing so. For example, giving each student a computer (or access to a computer) may allow us to pretend that our education system is up to date and aligned with technological progress. But this, of course, misses the real issue: what these students use their computer for.

And if that doesn't work, there is of course strategy number two: adopt the belief that the most important thing is for these young people to be happy, not to learn something that may serve them well later in life. Adopting this view obviously takes the pressure to act away and thus closes the gap.

An even bigger issue is the environmental problem. Again, one way to deal with the knowing-doing gap is to adopt the belief that the current climate change is simply part of a natural cycle and has absolutely nothing to do with human behaviour. But if that doesn't work for you, you may find comfort in carbon trading schemes that really just delay the day of reckoning. What about when we run out of carbon sequestration options? And can we really plant enough additional trees to off-set even just the burning of rain forests and extensive logging around the world? But these and other schemes give us a feeling of doing something, even though they are unlikely to truly address the fundamental environmental problems we have created—and continue to create.

Wherever we look, we seem to be caught in the knowing-doing gap. Why? Possibly the main reason is that our brain is not wired to take action today for benefits in the future. Our frontal lobes do allow us to understand how trends and developments impact on future conditions, creating sometimes deadly consequences. However, our frontal lobes are relatively new and, when it comes to acting, we rely on our 'older', more primitive brain that has been finetuned by nature over millions of years to address immediate needs. Put simply, when you get hungry you go out and hunt. When hunting grounds don't offer the returns needed, you move.

How often have we heard how people facing serious *immediate* threats have shown amazing resilience, ingenuity and determination in dealing with these situations? That's what our brains are designed to do. But we still have to learn to deal with the knowing-doing gap if we want to build a future rather than just find ways of dealing with today.

The fat smoker

Let's close this chapter with a reference to Maister's masterful book on how to close the knowing-doing gap.[2] Maister, a leading consultant to major professional services firms, smoked a packet a day and was overweight.

---

2   D Maister, *Strategy and the Fat Smoker: doing what's obvious but not easy*, Spangle Press, 2008.

He knew he needed to do something about it, but he didn't—until he had a heart attack.

Maybe it is not surprising that organisations are like people. After all, they are just a collection of human beings. We all know that we need to change the way we manage and work. But it is very difficult to make the change. Here are some of the conclusions Maister draws:

- It is hard to identify and create buy-in for what 'we' (the firm) should do if there is no strong sense of *we*.

- You don't have a purpose or mission (or a set of values) when you declare them. You have them when you put in place 'consequences for non-compliance'.

- Corporate culture is 'what you do when nobody is looking'.

- Marines have a special bond and a shared pride, built on shared values and a shared striving for excellence with integrity. Every marine grasps the concept of stewardship—the organisation, its reputation and its very effectiveness have been inherited from previous generations and are held in trust for future generations. They don't depend on a CEO presenting his personal values or ideas on how to take the organisation forward. We need to make shared values and rules for acceptable behaviour inherent in organisations, rather than expect organisations to simply adopt what successive CEOs demand.

- For individuals and organisations to succeed (to get done what they know they should be doing), they need to possess three things: passion, a sincere

interest in (and understanding of) people,
and principles.

We leave you with these thoughts and thank David Maister, one of the great consultants of our time, for his work.

KEY POINT

Just do it!

RECOMMENDED READING

Here are some informative books you might want to consider if you want to know more about particular topics covered in this publication.

Briggs, R and Stuart, G, *What Sticks: why most advertising fails and how to guarantee yours succeeds*, Kaplan Publishing, 2006.

Buchholz, A and Wördemann, W, *Spielstrategien im Business: Die Regeln des Wettbewerbs verändern*, Campus, 2008.

Christensen, CM, *The Innovator's Dilemma: when new technologies cause great firms to fail*, Harvard Business School Press, 1997.

Christensen, CM and Raynor, ME, *The Innovator's Solution: creating and sustaining successful growth*, Harvard Business School Press, 2003.

Christensen, CM, Anthony, SD and Roth, EA, *Seeing What's Next: using the theories of innovation to predict industry change*, Harvard Business School Press, 2004.

Duggan, W, *Strategic Intuition: the creative spark in human achievement*, Columbia Business School Publishing, 2007.

Häusel, HG (editor), *Neuromarketing: Erkenntnisse der Hirnforschung für Markenführung, Werbung und Verkauf*, Haufe, 2007.

Holt, D, *How Brands Become Icons*, Harvard Business School Press, 2004.

Johnson, S, *Everything Bad Is Good for You*, Penguin, 2006.

Klein, G, *Sources of Power: how people make decisions*, MIT Press, 1999.

Lafley, AG and Charan, R, *The Game-changer: how you can drive revenue and profit growth with innovation*, Crown/Random House, 2008.

Maister, D, *Strategy and the Fat Smoker: doing what's obvious but not easy*, Spangle Press, 2008.

Markides, CC, *Game-changing Strategies: how to create new market space in established industries by breaking the rules*, Wiley, 2008.

Martin, N, *Habit: the 95% of behavior marketers ignore*, FT Press, 2008.